Manufacturing
DEMAND

The Principles of Successful
Lead Management

David Lewis

Founder and CEO of DemandGen International

Manufacturing Demand
The Principles of Successful Lead Management
By David Lewis

© 2013 by New Year Publishing, LLC
144 Diablo Ranch Ct.
Danville, CA 94506 USA
http://www.newyearpublishing.com

ISBN 978-1-935547-37-2
Library of Congress Control Number:

To my two beautiful girls, Emily and Audrey,
who still laugh at my jokes and energize me with every hug.
You are the greatest gifts of my life.

On the factory floor, it's essential to ensure that all of the moving parts and machines work as a synchronized system, best exemplified by the gears that unify disparate functions. It's a similar story in demand generation as well. *Manufacturing Demand* focuses on the challenge of creating and maintaining continuous collaboration between sales and marketing teams—two gears of equal size and importance—to optimize revenue and profitability through a culture of partnership and synergy.

CONTENTS

FOREWORD

It was June 1978, the last day of school before my summer break would begin—ahh, no more studying, no more tests. I was a very happy 12-year-old. As I walked home, past the stores and shops on Ventura Boulevard, I could see workers unloading trucks packed with gear and setting up shelves for what would be Woodland Hills, California's, first-ever computer retail shop. I walked in and saw these TV-like monitors sitting on white cases with keyboards connected by curly cords. I had to know more.

"What are they?" I asked.

"They're computers," the guy in the blue suit replied. "IBM computers."

"So, what do they do?"

"A whole lot of things, son."

"Can you play games on them?"

"Well, sure. But you can also *make* games on them, too."

"Huh? How do you do that?"

"You'll have to read this to learn how."

He handed me a book on programming in the BASIC computer language, unwittingly setting my career in motion that very day. Day after day, I returned to the store to learn more and see more. I dove into the topic and started to develop a lifelong passion for technology and analytics. Fortunately, the father of one of my best friends—the controller for Max Factor, the make-up manufacturer—was an early buyer of the groundbreaking Apple II, which he used to create and manage VisiCalc spreadsheets from home after work. Watching him use the computer, I was more than intrigued—I was hopelessly hooked.

Soon, I was practically living at my friend's house, writing computer games on his dad's computer when he wasn't using it.

Within a year, I was begging my parents for my own computer—not exactly a common request for a teenager or a common household purchase in the '70s. Although they were convinced that I was merely going to write and play games, I somehow overcame their skepticism that this was a short-lived hobby. My father bought me an Apple IIe for high school and I was elated. For some kids, father-son memories might revolve around Norman Rockwell-like images of throwing a baseball or going to a favorite fishing hole. For me, my happiest day was going to the computer store with my dad to pick out the computer, a floppy-disk drive, and monitor, choosing a modem card, buying some essential software, and adding a graphics board. Once that Apple IIe came together, I had everything I needed to create and distribute my software. The only thing missing: the Internet.

To absolutely no one's surprise, this high-quality geek-time at home led me to choose computer science as my major when I enrolled in college in 1983. But something interesting happened to me along the way. After a few years of developing my own software, I realized that I enjoyed the posting and promoting of my software on electronic bulletin boards—even more than actually developing it. That realization led me to an even more important insight: *I liked interacting with people more than writing code for them.* And, although I was only a few courses shy of completing my requirements for a bachelor's degree in computer science, that crucial insight led me to switch my business major to marketing.

From there, as I'll explain in the pages that follow, my career has been a journey of discovery, from the creation of one of California's first Macintosh user groups in the 1980s to a series of positions with Microsoft, Farallon/Netopia, Ellie Mae, before starting DemandGen International in 2007. It has been an amazing journey that has enabled me to piece together my own unique perspective—and I encourage you to do the same in your own careers, fields, and endeavors.

Over the decades, I've had the good fortune to work with a broad cross-section of amazing colleagues and clients who have collectively helped me and the team at DemandGen devise and refine a unique methodology for cultivating and capitalizing on demand for products and services. But, of course, virtually every methodology or concept extends the work of those who've gone before and this book is no exception. I humbly stand on the shoulders of giants from such companies such as Concur, Taleo, NetApp, LinkedIn, Dell, American Express, Citrix, Apple, Microsoft, Cisco, Workday, Riverbed, Advent, Vistage, Marketo, Salesforce.com, Eloqua, Covidien, GAIN Capital, Novell, Shore-Tel, FICO, DuPont, SuccessFactors, and countless others. I hope that, in some humble ways, this book amplifies and extends their groundbreaking work.

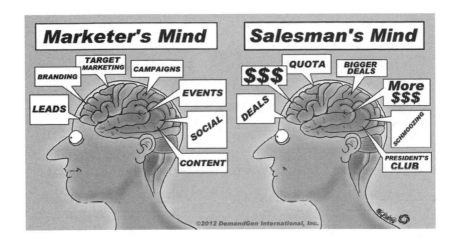

Chapter 1

THE TRANSFORMATION OF MARKETING

Marketing? Well, how hard can *that* be? I mean, that's just a bunch of "creative" people who sit around and brainstorm great ideas, right? They're the guys and gals who write clever headlines and draw up eye-popping graphics. They write the jingles we can't get out of our heads. They make billboards and glossy ads in magazines. They're the artists of the business world.

If that clichéd view of marketing was ever even true, it certainly isn't today. Don Draper's mythical, idealized image of photo shoots, genius sloganeers, big budgets, and office cocktails has long since given way to new and unforgiving reality.

In almost every way imaginable, marketing is in the midst of a dramatic transformation that is rewriting the rules of how brands engage with prospects and customers. The pages that follow document the key steps of the transformation. Is that art or is it science? As always, the answer is: a little of both. Today, however, the ratio of art to science is the inverse of what we've grown accustomed to. Previously, marketing was once primarily about the art of telling stories to vast segments of people. The emphasis was on delivering high concepts in a one-way monologue—and hoping for a response. The "science" component typically involved little more than loosely grouping audiences into vaguely defined demographic segments and judging results according to a few crude metrics.

Today, that ratio has been inverted. I certainly don't mean to diminish the excellence of creative marketing teams—their work has only improved over time. In fact, the creative tools available to marketing now enable the creation of stunning illustrations, animation, multimedia, and interactive media. But the rise of analytical precision in marketing has created unprecedented opportunities for companies to bring a greater level of scientific precision and repeatable, scalable processes to their marketing efforts. Just as a traditional factory can repeatedly and consistently convert raw materials into finished goods, a modern marketing process can apply a range of analytical disciplines, software tools, and other concepts and components to convert its demand-generation activities into a factory of sorts—"to manufacture demand."

DON'T BELIEVE THE BULL

But this is only a fairly recent phenomenon. When I was in college—after I transferred from computer science to the marketing department at California State University at Northridge—I had the absolute pleasure of studying advertising with Prof. Jerry Rosen, a gifted practitioner and executive at a leading Los Angeles advertising agency. One of the many things I loved about his course was the way he brought "real-life" cases and actual client work from his agency into our classroom. And, in my last semester as I prepared to start my career, Jerry's agency was hired by a leading trade association for the beef industry, seeking to boost its image. In the late '80s, beef was under competitive pressure from chicken, while pork was considered nutritional anathema, thanks to its association with fat and cholesterol.

Jerry asked each of us to prepare two conceptual campaigns to promote the beef industry. It would be my last major academic exercise before I joined the world of three-martini lunches. My first concept was very edgy, to say the least, with an R-rated slogan: "Don't Beat The Meat" (Hey, my only defense is this: I was in college and days away from graduating.) The concept drew a lot of laughs and positive feedback from classmates—and even from Jerry—for its attention-grabbing effect and connection with meat being unjustly attacked. But Jerry also knew that, as clever as that was, the client certainly wasn't going to approve anything so edgy.

So I showed my second concept, "Don't Believe All the Bull About Beef." It was another response to the beef-bashing taking place and emphasized the positive aspects of beef. I altered the classic butcher's diagram showing all of the various cuts of beef to highlight benefits like "High in iron." It was a class winner and I was feeling good about my ad skills—and my future—as Jerry summoned me for a quick conversation at the end of class. I was excited and even wondered if he was going to offer me a job at his agency. Expense-account lunches, here we come!

It was a brief, but very pivotal, conversation that affected my future in ways I had no way of grasping at the time. "David," he said, "you're a great adman with a lot of potential. But I have a counterintuitive suggestion for you: When you graduate, go find a sales job." I paused and looked at him. I certainly wasn't expecting that advice. He added, "Go into sales and learn *why* people buy. It will make you a much, much better marketer. Sales and marketing are two parts of the same army. Sales is the infantry and marketing is the air force, providing the air cover they need to achieve their goals. To be a great marketer, David, you first need to learn the buying process that sales facilitates."

It would have been easy to ignore this advice—and it was tempting to just go straight to an agency. But I decided that Jerry knew a whole hell of a lot more about this stuff than I did. Like Bill Murray's character Carl Spackler in *Caddyshack*, I figured, "I'll get into this sales dude's pelt and crawl around for a while." Instead of looking for the marketing job I had planned to pursue, I started scouring the area for sales jobs. And, as luck would have it, a tremendous opportunity arose.

Along with Alan Horowitz, a program manager with Hughes Aircraft, I had co-founded one of the first user groups devoted to the Apple Macintosh user community in Los Angeles. We brought together all kinds of Mac enthusiasts from across Southern California to learn about the latest in Mac technology and to share tips and techniques. At that time—the late 1980s—so many IT pros from aerospace and entertainment (the bedrock of SoCal industry) were coming to our meetings. Alan's job was to find vendors to speak to our group and, for one meeting, he asked Microsoft to demonstrate the latest versions of its word processing and spreadsheet programs—Word and Excel—to our members. But the company demurred because, rather amazingly, there was no Microsoft sales rep for the region. So Alan boldly told his contact at Microsoft headquarters, "I've got the guy for you—and he's graduating in a couple of weeks."

Just two weeks after collecting my diploma, there I was—the newest member of Microsoft's U.S. Sales and Marketing Division, which was about to launch Microsoft Windows 1.0. I was hired because I knew how to demonstrate the advantages of a graphical user interface, thanks to my experiences with the Macintosh user group since 1984. But what was more important and impressive to me was the division I was in: sales *and* marketing. Microsoft was progressive enough to understand that these functions were intertwined and needed to operate under unified leadership. Little did I know how quickly Jerry's advice would pay off.

OPENING DOORS IS EASY, CHANGE IS HARD

My region was the San Fernando Valley, home to the aerospace giants like Lockheed-Martin, Rockwell, and Hughes Aircraft. These companies were the Googles and Facebooks of their era. They had the budgets, the buzz, and the top talent of their generation. There I was, a 22-year-old sales rep with my 20-pound laptop and brick-sized cell phone, calling on the IT organizations of these great companies. And that's who you had to talk to. If you wanted to sell technology to the accounting department, you didn't talk to the accountants. You talked to IT, which set the standards and led the buying committees.

To my delight, I found that when you said, "Hello, I'm from Microsoft," you could actually get Lockheed's top IT man on the phone. He'd take my call and let me come in for an in-person meeting. I'd offer to demonstrate the next generation of the computer operating system and doors would open. That was the easy part.

Then, I'd open up that big laptop and explain the features and benefits of what would be the industry-changing innovation of Windows: visual charts in Excel, what-you-see-is-what-you-get editing in Word, and so much more. And they'd all sit around the table and nod sagely in agreement that this was a vast improvement over anything they were using.

And then we'd have to drop the bomb.

"Oh, by the way, to get this, you'll need to throw away all of your current computers and get new ones to run this operating system with more processing power, more memory, more disk space. Oh, and you'll need to retrain virtually every employee in the company. But don't worry—*you'll be better off.*" It was truly great to be so naïve at age 22. I hadn't a *clue* about the tremendous costs incurred or disruptions that would happen if they followed my advice. But it didn't take me long to recognize that getting past those initial appointments and facilitating the buying process was going to take time. Opening the doors was easy, but the change we were recommending was profoundly difficult.

In 1989, the Long Beach Grand Prix was taking place and Microsoft was holding a conference in the area. I had the good fortune to be invited to dinner with my boss and Microsoft founder Bill Gates. Like a good CEO, Bill asked a nice open-ended question: "How are things going, Dave?" And I spent the next few minutes explaining how satisfying it was that I could call any company in my territory and get an appointment with the right people. It was an honor to work for a company that had that kind of clout. But then I gingerly explained that, despite the strong appeal of our products and impact of our marketing messages, there were major challenges in getting prospects to standardize on three different products, which would inevitably create a lengthy sales cycle. I hesitated, but then finally had to express my concerns: "I am not sure we'll be closing accounts two to four weeks after a demo."

Quite simply, I'd learned a fundamental truth: Marketing can attract people to a message and generate interest and inquiries. But converting interest into a closed sale is a complex process and can be extremely challenging when paradigm-shifting products are introduced.

Gates looked at me and said, simply, "You're absolutely right. It's going to take time for these companies to change. But Windows will be the operating system of the future. Our sales people need to channel those objections back to marketing so they can develop the tools for you to overcome them, but overcome them we will." Bill was more than a technology visionary. He clearly saw that sales and marketing must be an integrated team in the battle for market share.

Over the next two years, the excitement over Windows continued to build. Our division ran an impressive "air war" ranging from large executive briefings to massive print advertising campaigns—and the messages resonated with our prospects. For "Demo Days," we'd set up tents in the parking lots of Hughes and Lockheed and their employees would take a break from their schedules and walk out to our tents, just to see these new products. That's some pretty strong interest. But conversion was nonetheless a drawn-out affair.

It was at one of these Demo Days where I met people from Farallon, the makers of the legendary PhoneNet product that basically created the market for networking over telephone wire. Despite many successes, I'd been feeling a bit caged-in during my two years at Microsoft—I only had 15 named accounts to call on and I was eager to unleash my "inner marketer." Farallon was seeking to recruit someone to handle the entire Southwestern U.S.—seven states in total—and they wanted someone to do both sales *and* business development. I grabbed the opportunity.

My father—always a source of sage wisdom—had long advised me to get a position working at a company headquarters and, in September 1991, Farallon offered me an opportunity I couldn't resist. I was named the regional manager for the Northwest, the company's largest region, which meant relocation to headquarters. At the time, Farallon was the leader in Macintosh networking, but independent Apple retailers were rapidly disappearing (these were the days before Apple would rewrite the rules for computer retailing). Mail order was quickly becoming the main sales channel for the company, and, in my role, I handled our largest channel accounts, which included the mail-order catalogs and distributors. This move marked an important transition in my career—one I enjoyed immensely—as I now had a marketing role and responsibility for our mail-order advertisements, messaging, imagery, offers, and more.

Fortunately, sales took off. Our mail-order ads did very well and we moved a ton of products. It was tremendously satisfying to finally apply the advertising and marketing skills I'd learned in college—and succeed.

In 1994, Farallon's vice president of marketing resigned and Ken Lamneck, our vice president of sales, took over the marketing operation as well. He said to me, "Dave, you've done a great job with sales, business development, the mail-order channel and you have a knack for this marketing stuff. How about taking the job as director of marketing?" Clearly, I'd have never been considered for a role like this if I'd walked in off the street with my sales resume and just a degree in marketing. As our vice president of sales and marketing, Ken liked that I saw both disciplines as an integrated function and was willing to take a bet on me.

THE FIFTH AND SIXTH P'S OF MARKETING—
AND THE RISE OF THE MARKETING GEEK

So what did I do next? What any marketer was doing in 1994: I ran to the bookstore and bought as many books on marketing as I could find. I worried that anything I'd learned in school was hopelessly outdated by then. And there was this new phenomenon called the "World Wide Web" that was sure getting a lot of attention, and I knew I would somehow have to figure out how that should factor into Farallon's marketing mix. But these were early days for the Web (many conferences featured passionate discussions on where your website's navigation should be placed and best practices in banner-ad creation).

Unfortunately, the market for "pure Apple" products was withering—Microsoft Windows was dominating the business market. If we stayed loyal to the Mac market, we'd likely go out of business. So we decided to take our plug-and-play networking expertise and design a solution to let small businesses connect to this "Internet thing." We'd also offer the first cross-platform remote-control solution. We rebranded the company "Netopia" and planned to launch our remote-control product—Timbuktu—for the PC market and new Internet access equipment for small businesses.

Marketing strategy? Well, since there wasn't going to be any additional budget, my grand strategy was to use the Web—and only the Web—as our entire channel for marketing, lead-generation, e-commerce, and support—a fairly audacious choice in 1994, well before any best practices existed for using the Web in this way. While our competitors—primarily Norton and Symantec—were focusing on so-called "road warriors," we believed Timbuktu would be ideally suited to the IT help desk professional and we took great pains to identify who he was in complete detail—his pain points, his needs, and which Timbuktu features would be more appealing to him than competing products. All my experience calling on IT teams at Microsoft really helped me know this audience inside and out. I worked with product marketing, sales, and my marketing team to understand the profile of these buyers and users. I might not have realized it at the time, but building these buyer personas—and getting it right—was a crucial milestone. My goal was for all of us to have a shared view of the customer so we could properly attract them and sell to them.

Next, we built landing pages and forms, and that necessitated something I hadn't expected: a lot—and I mean a LOT—of cooperation with our peers in IT who controlled our database and website updates. We needed their help to build those forms and backend databases and move records to our own homegrown customer relationship management (CRM) system. At the time, we didn't have any formal commercial-software infrastructure and SaaS didn't exist yet. Instead, we had to walk down the halls to partner with our two new sets of friends: sales and IT. Let's face it: in school, these might not have been the guys who sat at my lunch table. But now? Now, they were going to be my wingmen. That was a very informative experience for me—it opened my eyes to the need for and potential of technology to improve marketing. My background in computer science helped quite a bit as I was "trusted" by the IT people because I could talk their language and deliver clear requirements integrating the website, e-commerce, and our customer database.

Fortunately for us, Timbuktu became a phenomenal success and dominated the help-desk market. The sales of our Internet access equipment also skyrocketed. And all of our results were driven solely from Web-based marketing—no print advertising, no tradeshows, no direct mail. Our website forms captured buyer persona information and we only sent qualified leads to sales—the rest were nurtured and driven to our online store. Netopia went public in 1996, and, in three years, the stock went from $7 to $90. Our marketing budget didn't increase though. It didn't need to. We actually *decreased* our spending because we knew exactly which channels worked and which didn't. Bottom line: The Internet was far more efficient at demand generation than traditional mass marketing and, for the first time in my career, I could really measure marketing's impact on revenue.

Based on these results, I recognized that the classic "Four P's of Marketing"—product, price, place, and promotion—weren't quite complete. From my perspective, marketing needed two more P's: Process and Programming

- *Process*—There can be many different definitions here, but it largely involves identifying and mapping the entire buying process, from awareness to transaction, including the various buying stages. Who does the buyer interact with? How do they "on-board"? What process does the buyer go through to become a customer?

- *Programming*—This means instrumenting a series of previously manual processes using automated tools. To be effective today, marketing <u>must</u> automate as many portions of its process as possible, for example, lead capture, scoring, nurturing, and the passing of data among various company systems.

In particular, it's that last P—Programming—that gave rise to what I call (with tremendous respect and affection) "the marketing geek." He (or she) is the go-to person *within* marketing who understands the tools and analytics that are needed today. In 1992, marketing had to rely on a Web developer or another department. By 2008, the mantra was "Geek is Chic" and many forward-thinking marketing departments had a designated staff person with the aptitude and interest in systems and analytics—the person who enjoys codifying over creativity.

Today, it's not unthinkable to expect we'll soon see an executive-level person—call her the Chief Marketing Technologist—who will oversee this crucial discipline. Marketing has experienced such dramatic and profound change in the last 20 years—it's only natural that corporate structures should change as well. More than ever, marketing needs the geeks—the people who can understand and manage marketing automation, who understand search-engine optimization, social media platforms, and CRM.

The classic Four P's were about products and the *art* of marketing. But these two new P's are really about the *science* of marketing—about building a machine to capture leads, automate the movement of data through the funnel, analyze that data for smarter decisions and processes, connect to sales systems, and demonstrate the value you're producing from marketing activities and investments.

And that's a long way from Don Draper's wet bar and cigarette lighter.

Chapter 2

ARE YOU READY TO START MANUFACTURING DEMAND?

There's a new mandate in today's global economy: We're now in an age where we must *manufacture demand*. Here's what I mean. Until the 20th century, a producer—whether a blacksmith or a baker—produced only sufficient quantities of his goods that he could sell (often through custom orders). In most instances, because of perishability, thin profit margins, or an inability to reach more remote/distant markets, he didn't make much of anything beyond what he *knew* he could sell (or had pre-sold).

But then a new generation of men at the dawn of the last century fashioned entirely new ideas about how to produce goods. It was the birth of the Industrial Age, and one of the most profound consequences was that companies developed the ability to produce more goods than they could sell in their local market. That meant they needed ways to spread the word about their products and services—which dovetailed with the emergence of mass media. Today, with a global economy, air travel, and instantaneous communication and commerce, the marketing and sales process needs to happen everywhere, simultaneously.

As a result, savvy marketers are taking automation principles from the industrial age and applying them to the information age. By leveraging new technologies and applying a "factory mentality," progressive companies are embracing a new way to ***manufacture demand***—and its resulting revenue. In this analogy—which underpins much of this book—the sales and marketing function is one integrated factory where raw demand that's generated at the top of the funnel (from inbound and outbound marketing initiatives) proceeds along an efficient production line through defined stages where different functions are performed to maximize conversions into revenue-producing customers.

Unfortunately—perhaps as a consequence of the highly successful "division of labor" concept that had sparked the Industrial Age—the sales and marketing functions became very distinct and separate functions. In some industries, that was tolerable and acceptable because a business model for a complex, highly differentiated product (say, a surgical device) might be very sales-centric. But in other segments (e-commerce dot-com companies come to mind), there are no salespeople whatsoever—marketing *is* sales. Between these two extremes, however, lies a vast middle ground where sales and marketing teams need to work hand-in-hand to achieve their common goals: more sales and more revenue.

So what's this book about? In a nutshell, it's about aligning sales and marketing functions from a variety of perspectives. It starts with processes and systems and moves to culture. It's a journey with many milestones along the way. Yes, it's a truism: marketing is from Mars and sales is from Venus, but by understanding and embracing the differences, we can leverage each's strengths and create a "1 + 1 = 3" dynamic that delivers disproportionate value.

How do you achieve that alignment? For marketers, it starts with a willingness to immerse yourself in the company's sales process. Do some "ride-alongs" where you accompany some sales reps when they call on customers. Go *interview* customers. Sit in their offices. *Ask* why they purchased, what the process was like, and who was involved. *Talk* to your counterparts in sales—regularly. *Ask* how work is going, how the trade show was, and how they define a lead.

I was fortunate enough to embark on my journey toward alignment by starting my career in a B2B sales role at Microsoft. If you've not done your tour of duty in sales, then ride along with some top sales reps for a few days at a minimum and gain some invaluable insight into the buying process. Trust me: It will do more for your career than an MBA in marketing.

There are ways to facilitate that alignment. Let's call them the "Five Principles of Lead Management." The following several pages introduce these principles at a summary level. Subsequent chapters delve into each topic in greater detail. It's important to realize that, while these chapters are presented in a useful sequence, your route on the journey may vary. These principles are not sequential steps and you can approach your marketing challenges from any of these entry points.

Equipping Your "Marketing Factory"—The Essential Importance of Marketing Automation Systems

Just as automation rewrote the rules for production in the Industrial Age, marketing automation tools and CRM systems have opened the door to unprecedented efficiencies, speed, and scale. These systems are *a non-negotiable requirement* for a contemporary marketing organization seeking to implement the principles of this book: a Demand Funnel, lead scoring, lead nurturing, and more.

Note, to many, the terms "marketing automation" and "email marketing" were, at least preliminarily, synonymous. If that was ever true, it's certainly not today. The primitive days of "batch and blast" are over. Where email marketing initially emerged as a way to send out one-time messages to influence impulse/consumer purchases, marketing automation is designed to support complex cycles that involve multiple touches over longer periods of time. Instead of creating "spam cannons," marketing automation enables us to create orchestrated campaigns that target specific buyer roles with specific content at defined stages of a buying cycle. Marketing automation is the engine that manages that complex process.

Integrating marketing automation with customer relationship management (CRM) systems raises the power of each component significantly. These technologies are the foundation of achieving that all-important alignment: creating a centralized location for all leads and marketing activity.

If your organization is like most, chances are you have a CRM system such as Salesforce, or perhaps a homegrown system. Marketing automation (MA) is rapidly following the same adoption curve as CRM. It has reached the "early majority" phase of its product lifecycle—about 20 percent market penetration—and there's little doubt that some form of MA system will eventually be in place at virtually every B2B or sizable B2C business in the next few years, even if it's nothing more than a souped-up version of Microsoft Outlook. Most likely, it'll be considered one of the top five SaaS applications of the first decade of the 21st century.

While there are already multiple options to choose from when it comes to marketing automation and CRM tools, it is not the goal of this book to tell you which one is best or even advise you how to go about selecting the right tool. Hence, you won't see a chapter devoted to the topic. The key point here is that you need to get a marketing automation system if you want to out-market your competition. I'm serious. It's not a matter of IF you need one. It's time.

PRINCIPLE NO. 1:
BUILDING BUYER PERSONAS—WHO BUYS AND WHY?

Too often, sales and marketing focus only on the negative feedback from sales about lead quality. But sometimes, the sub-text is more meaningful. The friction arises because the two groups don't actually agree on the fundamentals: What is a lead? Who are the buyers? Why are they buying? Clarifying these matters is a necessity before you can embark on manufacturing demand.

The best way to get that alignment underway is to develop a holistic *persona*—a detailed character study—for each of the various buyer participants—and then to act on that knowledge to deliver the right content at the right time to *assist* the buyer through the buying process. But you have to know *who* that buyer is. Let me explain that with a real-world example: mine.

In 2004, a few years after leaving Netopia, I took on the role of vice president of marketing for Ellie Mae, now the leading supplier of mortgage-banking software. Its first software product was about to be launched, and the company wanted a seasoned software marketer to come in and crush competitors that held 80-percent market share. It was a tough challenge, no doubt, but it was an excellent opportunity to implement a marketing process methodology and the kind of programmatic infrastructure I had deployed at Netopia.

At that time, CRM and marketing automation solutions were just starting to hit the market, and I was excited by what I saw emerging from the vendors' labs. When I arrived, Ellie Mae, a sizeable software enterprise, was using a $35 shareware program for email marketing and had no landing pages on its website to capture a single lead. So we had a lot of opportunity—*and* a lot of work. But before I implemented my strategy to redesign the website into a lead-generation machine and use the marketing tactics I'd learned, I knew I wanted to forge the strongest possible relationship with my counterpart in sales, Joe Langner.

Joe was an absolute stud at getting new customers and I wanted to know how he did it at Ellie Mae—so that I could gain insight into the mind of the buyer, uncover the messaging that led to his successes, and apply them to marketing.

Let's face facts: Sales guys like to go to lunch, right? So I took Joe to his favorite sushi place—regularly—and quizzed him relentlessly. Who did he sell to? Who approved the purchases? Why did they buy our product? Why did they buy from competitors? What could improve? Where did the sales process tend to slow down? I wanted Joe to tell me as much as he could about the various buyer participants so that I could shape our marketing activities to pursue that buyer persona.

Then, I persuaded Joe to let me accompany him on sales calls for at least a month. The first day seemed like a scene from Denzel Washington's 2001 film *Training Day*. We rode from client to client as he mentored me like a rookie cop. (Fortunately, we didn't have a gun battle with him trying to kill me and me killing him like in the movie.)

This scenario exemplifies marketing and sales alignment in action—and that means a whole lot more than integrating software or drawing flow charts. It's a deeper alignment that results when two teams work closely to forge shared, mutual agreements and understanding of each other's role in the process. Yes, getting the right leads to sales is important. But it's just as important to ensure sales picks up right where marketing hands off, in a seamless, synchronized, frictionless fashion.

Yes, that time in the field was great for building a rapport with Joe and learning about the sales process and messaging. But almost as importantly, I met the people we were selling to. I met Gary, the broker owner and Maria, the loan processor. I learned their pain points, what motivated them, and why they buy—and let me tell you, it wasn't what was listed under "features" on the current product slicks.

In Chapter 3, I'll cover buyer personas in greater detail.

PRINCIPLE NO. 2: THE DEMAND FUNNEL

The Demand Funnel is a systematic framework for aligning and grouping similar prospective customers and tracking their progress as they gradually move through their buying process. Creating this funnel should be a joint exercise of sales and marketing and is a tremendously important catalyst for achieving that all-important alignment.

Using a defined, agreed-upon vocabulary, the sales and marketing teams bridge any differences to specify what constitutes a lead, establish the various funnel milestones, and then assign meaning, ownership, and process to each stage of the funnel. In Chapter 4, we'll discuss a useful taxonomy and how to operationalize those definitions into a working Demand Funnel.

The Four Key Marketing Technologies for Manufacturing Demand

- **The website**—Turbocharge this lead-capture machine with fresh content and easy navigation.

- **Marketing automation system**—This powerful tool executes your campaigns, houses your lead-scoring system, automates your lead-nurture programs, and measures marketing's contribution to revenue.

- **Customer relationship management system**—In many ways, CRM is the yin-yang of marketing automation. It's the interface for sales to interact with the *same data* used by marketing to manage leads, customers, and opportunities.

- **Marketing analytics software**—Analytics may be bundled into the MA or CRM system—that might suffice. Or you might require a separate business intelligence tool, depending on the complexity of your systems and your analytical needs.

PRINCIPLE NO. 3: LEAD SCORING

Once you have a Demand Funnel, you need to rate the various contacts in there. What's an A-level lead vs. a B- or C-level lead? Again, this process will involve significant collaboration between sales and marketing.

Who is your ideal prospect? What does he say or do to indicate he's ready to buy? In other words, what are the *characteristics* and the *behaviors* (chiefly, although not exclusively online) that define the likelihood that a prospect will purchase your product/service? How do those various characteristics combine to form a lead score? One thing we must clearly understand: a lead score is NOT a forecast of who will buy. It's a prioritized to-do list for sales.

Companies can use a variety of scoring models including *interest-only*, *qualification-only*, and *a two-dimensional* combination of interest and qualification. A newer method, *predictive lead scoring*, uses data mining to find subtle historical patterns that are also excellent indicators of fitness and interest.

In Chapter 5, we'll talk about lead scoring in significant detail and show you how to determine if it's paying off by using some simple ROI calculations.

PRINCIPLE NO. 4: LEAD NURTURING

Just because a lead doesn't obediently proceed at our desired pace through all stages of our defined Demand Funnel doesn't mean the prospect doesn't have significant value. The fact is, every buyer requires different information and messages at different stages of the Demand Funnel. We need to have the right content at the right time and at the right frequency to coax that prospect through the buying process. That's what lead nurturing is designed to do.

Lead nurturing is a two-way dialogue with prospects at each stage of the buying process (Demand Funnel) to help the buyer achieve his objectives. There are an almost limitless number of nurtures—seed nurturing to add new names to the Demand

Funnel, inquiry nurtures, marketing qualified lead (MQL) nurtures, special purpose nurtures, and even post-purchase, recycling, and reengagement nurtures. We'll explain these in more detail in Chapter 6. We'll also spend some time covering content (or "lead bait") strategies for various nurtures.

PRINCIPLE NO. 5: ANALYTICS

The newly emerging science—the process and programming—of demand generation affords us unprecedented opportunities to pinpoint key prospects and deliver finely tuned messages at just the right time.

But this discipline of measuring this machine's performance not only gauges the overall effectiveness of our marketing strategy, it also generates the right data to help us assess the effectiveness of campaigns that make up that strategy. Marketing automation not only processes and leverages data, but also generates vast amounts of data that we can analyze to refine and improve marketing performance:

- **Key Performance Indicators**—These are the analytics reviewed by senior managers.

- **Operational Statistics**—Here, we see the performance of the lead management framework—how many inquiries are at the top of the funnel? How much qualified lead volume is moving through? What are the outputs (*e.g.* conversions to closed-won business)?

- **Tactical Metrics**—Here's where we measure campaign effectiveness using stats like landing-page conversion, click-through rates, the performance of touches in our nurture program, best lead sources, offer consumption rates and more.

That marketing geek starts to matter more and more. If you don't have an inner geek to let out, go hire one or seek an expert. We'll go into more depth in Chapter 7, but the fundamentals of marketing analytics can be boiled down to what I call the "Three C's":

- What can you *Count*?—What data is available to you, and how does your demand generation process capture it? Pay greater attention to the metrics that can yield insights on what's working and what isn't.

- What *Counts*?—Not everything you *can* count is *worth* counting. Don't waste time on red-herring data that doesn't illuminate your marketing or business challenges.

- Can you *Count* on it?—Is the data reliable? Is it captured consistently and automatically? Is it data that results from a repeatable process so it will always be there to measure and incorporate in reports and dashboards? Consistency is key. Your CFO doesn't come in with a different set of reports every week. I've learned over the years that everything trends no matter how you measure it—unless you can't consistently measure it.

In the following chapters, we will explore these principles in greater depth. But the one vital step to success—one that's more about psychology than systems—is to build that all-important rapport with sales. Continuing our factory analogy, it's important to remember that the "factory workers"—your marketing *and sales* teammates—are a single function spread across two departments.

Demand Generation = Sales + Marketing.

It's one equation, one integrated process. But to make this process work, the individuals in both functional groups must *want* to be culturally aligned and must *see* themselves as a unified team.

Pay attention and nurture the culture. Create a shared vision and shared incentives, and form a constant dialogue between the teams. Happy hours and TGIFs are a good start and go a long way in team building—just don't invite HR.

KEY TAKEAWAYS

- A new factory mentality—"manufacturing demand"—is emerging that leverages new technologies and integrates the sales and marketing functions into a unified, aligned team.

- Manufacturing demand requires a foundation of marketing automation and customer relationship management.

- There are five principles to manufacturing demand:
  - Buyer personas
  - The Demand Funnel
  - Lead scoring
  - Lead nurturing
  - Analytics

- Demand Generation = Sales + Marketing

Chapter 3

BUYER PERSONAS: WHO ARE YOU TALKING TO?

When you're manufacturing demand, you have to start with raw materials, and in this case that means prospects—lots of them. The best way to communicate with a prospect is by starting with a very clear picture or *persona* of the ideal customer. You can't communicate effectively—in any context—until you know exactly who you're communicating *with*. Without knowing who that person is, you have a very limited ability to gauge and take measure of the recipient of your communication.

You can't effectively calibrate your message, voice, content, timing, and other essentials of good communication. In this chapter, we'll learn about identifying your buyer, developing a persona for each buyer so that you can automate one-to-one communications, using their online behaviors to identify quality candidates, supplementing your understanding with well-chosen third-party data, and providing timely and relevant content that corresponds to each stage of the buying cycle.

In a buying environment that's increasingly characterized (at least in preliminary stages) by online anonymity as buyers peruse information and resources without identifying themselves, it's becoming very difficult to simply know who the buyer is. That anonymity also creates content challenges because today's buyer will consume content not only on your company's website but from countless third-party sources. He'll scan all over the Web for information about your products and services. He'll do Twitter searches. He'll consult social media friends. He'll read the user reviews. He'll take in the industry trade publications or independent research. And all of that research is often taking place before you even know who this prospective buyer is. You don't have much control over that. But what you *can* control is the content that you produce and syndicate yourself.

And, of course, before you can produce that content, you need to know a fair bit about who will consume that content. In concert with your counterparts in sales, you need to develop rich buyer personas that capture the "buying backstory" about typical prospective buyers.

But what is a *buyer persona*? It's a fictional character that you develop to represent a targeted demographic type—a typical customer or prospect. It is usually more effective if you can humanize the persona and almost bring it to life. Building a buyer persona for marketing is much like developing a character for a novel or a movie. The difference is that you're not really making anything up from scratch—your buyers already exist. You're just defining the specifics for an individual "average" buyer.

THE BUYING COMMITTEE

Of course, you need to see and understand that buyer in context. For B2B *considered* purchases, that often means some form of buying committee. Who has a place at the table when it comes to making purchasing decisions? Who typically holds the most sway in these matters? Users? Technical buyers? Economic buyers? Where do they get their information? What do they rely on and value? Who are their peer groups?

These aren't easy questions to answer, and that's where your alignment and partnership with sales becomes crucial. Your sales counterparts will play a critical role in helping you identify and flesh out these personas. It's essential that sales and marketing have a fundamental level of agreement in establishing these personas.

THE STAGES OF THE BUYING CYCLE

Once you believe you've successfully identified and articulated the key roles on the buying committee, it's time to work with the stages of your buying cycle. The abbreviation AIDA was coined by American advertising and sales pioneer E. St. Elmo Lewis in 1898 to describe the consumer's buying process: Attention—Interest—Desire—Action. Today, our understanding of this process has evolved into five stages: need recognition, information search, evaluation of alternatives, purchase decision, and post-purchase behavior.

Now, you needn't rigidly adhere to these stages—your business model may dictate other approaches. In fact, I'd like to suggest a further refinement of these phases, a framework that can work for any non-impulse purchase—B2B or B2C—that involves some level of careful pre-purchase analysis. Let's call it **The Five Stages of Considered Purchases:**

- **Inquire**—Is there a solution to my problem or need?
- **Learn**—How does your solution solve my problem or need?
- **Evaluate**—Do I like your solution (and is it better than others)?
- **Justify**—Do I want your solution (over others)?
- **Select**—I am buying your solution.

CREATING THE PERSONAS

When you first sit down to work on persona development, it might seem more than a little daunting to stare at that blank sheet. If you're looking for some great ideas for defining personas, be sure to check out our Persona Development Tool in the resources area of this book's website (listed below). This template guides you through the process of creating a buyer persona and tees up questions to help you describe your ideal buyer. It's a basic format, allowing you to make your personas as simple or complex as your needs require. The template also provides some examples to help you understand how to complete the template. For our examples, we used the personas of a mortgage broker and a loan processor, which I used back when I was at Ellie Mae.

> *Be sure the visit the book's website*
> www.manufacturingdemand.com
> *for additional resources.*

I like to start by giving our imaginary person a name and supplying a (stock) photo. This really helps make this persona feel real, allowing us to more easily endow him or her with skills, experience, education, thoughts, and feelings.

- **The Profile Overview**—In the overview, imagine that you are telling a friend about this person. Is it typically a man or woman? What's the approximate age? What's his role? How does she spend her workday? Depending on your product or service, you may want to look at different kinds of attributes that tie more closely to the make-up of the ideal customer profile. The goal here is to build up a solid picture of this person that everyone can recognize.

- **Pain Points**—What does your prospect worry about? What does she wish she could change? Be sure to create your list from the prospect's point of view. Sometimes it helps to complete the following questions using that person's "voice":
  - I'm concerned about…
  - I don't have…
  - I worry about…
  - I wish…

- **Key Drivers/Motivators**—These are the issues that mean the most to this person: the things that are behind every decision he makes, with particular emphasis on issues relating to your product/service. Complete these thoughts:
  - I want to …
  - I need to…
  - I must…

- **Role in the Buying Committee**—Is this person the decision-maker? An influencer? Who might influence this person?

- **Effective Influences**—What kind of content and information is most effective in communicating persuasively with this person? Are there particular kinds of information he is most likely to want? Is any one kind of media more effective than another? Is she likely to take advantage of any particular kinds of offers?

In the following example, we can see how a persona comes to life by the use of full and careful descriptions. Ellie Mae sells software to mortgage companies and this profile overview describes the primary decision maker—a mortgage broker:

GARY | MORTGAGE BROKER

Profile Overview

Gary is a licensed mortgage broker and is the owner of the business, similar in role and responsibilities to a CEO. He has responsibility for the overall company strategy, operations, and process establishment, and is typically heavily involved in sales and marketing activities for the firm.

Most brokerage firms are relatively small, so Gary is much like a traditional small business owner: concerned with the day-to-day activities, personnel, and the bottom line. He also functions as a loan officer, generating new business and serving his own set of clients. In common with the majority of mortgage broker/owners, who are male aged 30-55, Gary has about 15-20 years of experience in financial services.

Gary spends a portion of his workday networking with potential clients and driving new business. He also communicates with current clients, especially high-profile or high-value ones. He stays in touch with the loan officers and processors, monitoring their pipelines and ensuring that each loan is progressing as it should, stepping in to help when necessary.

By reading that, don't you have a bit more insight into who this decision maker is and how you might communicate with him? Not only that, going through this profiling process with sales to create a shared vision of the buyer is a great way to start the alignment process.

This simple grid—a "Buyer's Stage Table"—makes it easy to see how your messaging needs to change based on your prospect's stage in the buying cycle. First, you define your persona's motivation at each stage and what questions are being asked at that point. Then, you look at the right messages and value propositions that should be communicated at that stage, and what marketing medium is best. The following matrix shows you how to think about the persona for each phase of the buying cycle.

BUYER'S STAGE TABLE

	INQUIRE	LEARN	EVALUATE	JUSTIFY	SELECT
Define the persona's motivation at each stage.	What interests me?	What do I want to know?	What do I think?	Is this right? What else Is needed?	Am I ready to buy?
What questions is your persona asking at each stage?	Questions:	Questions:	Questions:	Questions:	Questions:
Define the key messages and value propositions	Messages:	Messages:	Messages:	Messages:	Messages:
What offers do they respond to?	Offer types:	Offer types:	Offer types:	Offer types:	Offer types:

In the next table, we see what a completed matrix might look like:

	INQUIRE	LEARN	EVALUATE	JUSTIFY	SELECT
Define the persona's motivation at each stage.	My current system is outdated and isn't working for me.	I want to see what's out there.	I need to compare the options.	I am leaning toward this product and want to make sure it's right.	I want this product and I want it up and running quickly.
What are the questions your persona is asking at each stage?	What are top mortgage companies using to run their businesses today?	How do these new systems work and how will they impact my business?	What are the key differences between these systems and what I currently have?	I am leaning toward this product, but is there anything else I should consider like training?	I want this product. What will it take to get it up and running quickly?
Define the key messages and value propositions.	This newer system lets you process more loans faster and make more profit per loan. If you want to comply with new lending laws, you need a system that helps you stay compliant.	These are the key benefits to you, the business owner, and how it supports you and your staff. It is affordable for your size of business and easy to use.	These demos and resources show benefits specific to your needs, such as how it improves your workday and allows for easy migration and deployment.	This solution is very popular and makes a lot of other businesses successful. It is a good investment.	You can take advantage of excellent deployment tools, service and support offerings, and training.

	INQUIRE	LEARN	EVALUATE	JUSTIFY	SELECT
What offers do they respond to?	Content that covers "success secrets of top mortgage firms."	Content that shows how these new systems will benefit them.	Online demos, webinars, and on-site presentations for larger mortgage firms. Free trials.	Case studies, testimonials, videos from both business owners and their staff, ROI calculator.	How-to guides, implementation tools, and training curriculum.

Persona development is a fascinating exercise to do with your team. You'll discover all kinds of new ideas and insights as you think about each facet of your buyer's personality.

"Psst...Hey, buddy. You want some fresh content?

MAPPING THE CONTENT

Now that we have roles/personas and stages of the buying cycle, you should build a simple matrix like the one shown in Figure 3.1 that maps your various content assets to the appropriate buying roles and stages. A completed matrix helps you spot content gaps. It will also help you plan your nurture content, so you know which content to use for each persona and when to use it based on the stage of the funnel they are in.

	INQUIRE	LEARN	EVALUATE	JUSTIFY	SELECT
User-Buyer					
Technical Buyer					
Economic Buyer					

Figure 3.1 Sample Content Workbook

HOW TO TAKE YOUR CONTENT TONE AND VOICE TO THE NEXT LEVEL

It's not my intention to make this a book about content generation. Books like *Made to Stick* handle those topics much more capably. But, when it comes to content development, there are still some universal principles that apply.

- **The One-to-One Connection**—It's important to remember the one-to-one connection because ultimately we're all marketing "B2I"—business to individual. We need to talk WITH buyers, not AT them. *All* forms of buying are eventually based on human interactions—and this remains true even though so much more of the buying activity is taking place outside the view of your sales and marketing team.

- **Start with "Why?"**—As author Simon Sinek said in his book *Start with Why*, Martin Luther King, Jr., didn't proclaim in his legendary speech, "I have a plan." He said, "I have a *dream*." Reaching your would-be buyer on an emotional level is far more effective than starting on a pragmatic level.

MANUFACTURING DEMAND IN ACTION
Citrix Online

Every month, more than 17,000 new customers begin to use Citrix Online's world-class collaboration tools to work from anywhere with anyone, saving them time and enabling them to get more done. Products such as GoToMyPC, GoToMeeting, and GoToAssist have redefined how people communicate and collaborate around the world. However, the use cases for these different products varies greatly, depending on the prospect's role within the prospect organization.

Citrix Online's product marketing team developed specific personas for each product and ensured that content assets were appropriate for each product and market segment. Prospects without an identified persona are tagged with persona values as they respond to various offers.

By building personas for each prospect who could use their solution for virtual conferencing and avoid costly, time-consuming travel, Citrix Online has dramatically improved the performance of its lead nurturing campaigns. Weekly campaigns have seen response rates rise significantly and Citrix Online achieved more than 100 percent of its assigned lead goals (compared to 90 percent before their persona-based marketing efforts).

"We realized that we needed to speak to the specific needs of our prospects," said Baxter Denney, Citrix Online's manager of database marketing. "With our personas, we can now send out content offers by persona and segment our marketing efforts to target appropriate groups with appropriate information at the appropriate time. As a result, we've enjoyed increased response rates, which is helping us meet revenue targets."

- **Use a Personal Tone**—We are all inundated by messaging every day, especially in our email inboxes. Messaging that's written for the masses will not engage your prospects. *Talking* to them—especially if you talk to the persona—will connect them to your message on a personal level. Too often, I see this type of writing: "Don't miss our webinar Monday at 1 p.m. on how our [product name] helps with regulatory compliance." Try this kind of tone instead: "We're holding a webinar for mortgage brokers next week on regulatory issues plaguing our industry. Can you join us? It's Monday at 1 p.m."

Remember: Avoid the temptation to continually focus on your company and your products. Think about the buyer's perspective, not your own. Don't be that guy who does all the talking on the first date!

OPERATIONALIZE THE PERSONAS

Since so much of the early-stage buying activity is self-directed by somewhat anonymous site visitors, we lose a crucial advantage: the ability to read the body language of the prospect. Any savvy retailer or experienced direct-sales rep develops a keen ability to recognize both explicit and implicit buying intentions just by watching and observing the buyer and his/her actions. A jewelry saleswoman can assess a prospect's buying intentions and facilitate the sales process when she has a prospect asking to try on pieces of jewelry or when she learns the prospect is shopping for a special occasion. A car salesman can size up a prospect's propensity to purchase and tailor his approach accordingly just by asking what type of car the person currently drives and if he bought or leased the car.

Fortunately, we can achieve similar (though derived) levels of insight by examining what author and Eloqua co-founder

Steve Woods, calls *digital body language*[1]—the so-called "mouse-trails" that are generated by our marketing automation systems by people visiting our websites, clicking emails, and submitting website forms. We can "see" and gauge the level of interest by analyzing such online metrics as:

- The number of website visits by that individual

- The key areas visited, such as pricing pages or product selectors

- The quality of the email address—is it from a "free" domain or a work domain?

- The number of pages visited. (The average is 2.5, so if the visitor is looking at, say, more than six pages, we can infer a high level of interest.)

- What terms they searched for to arrive at the site

- The types of assets downloaded

- The amount of time spent on the site

These types of measurable online behaviors help us identify someone who's moving through a buying cycle. How can you be sure? Correlate. Take your 10 most recent customers and "reverse-engineer" their online buying process by reviewing the key interactions with your website and content that's stored within your marketing automation system. From their first interaction through closed transaction, what did they do? If they are not atypical customers, their mousetrails will be fairly good indicators of behavior for who might purchase in the future.

To operationalize your personas—which means creating that persona in your database—you must identify the fields in your database that correspond to the characteristics of your personas. Each persona must have a unique combination of fields—things

---

[1] *Digital Body Language*, Steve Woods, New Year Publishing, 2008.

like role/title, industry, size of company, department, geography, and the other attributes specific to your personas.

How do you populate those fields—how do you get that data? You can obtain it in a couple of different ways. First, you can capture it when the prospect fills out a form. Let's pause and note that we must carefully think about the forms we present and where in the buying process we ask for data. Early in the buying cycle, it can be off-putting to ask for a lot of data. It's too soon. However, after the visitor has appeared a couple of times or has requested a higher-value content asset (e.g. an e-book or a free trial), it's entirely appropriate to ask for a few more bits of persona data.

We can infer some of this data from an IP address (and there are software tools that excel at this task). We can also infer some of the answers from the visitor's digital body language and by the nature of the content assets requested. Finally, we can supplement our own data with third-party information from external sources that integrate with your website, CRM, or marketing automation system.

Armed with a holistic, 360-degree view of the prospective buyer, you're in a much better position to understand the nuances and factors that subtly shape buying behavior and purchase decisions. You can begin to map online activity to specific roles—and then respond in a one-to-one fashion that creates true dialogue and engagement—not boring chest-thumping. Persona development takes time and patience—and don't be afraid to go back and continue to refine. Personas, in fact, should change regularly to stay in step with changes to your business and your market. Put in the effort early, and you'll find that the payoff down the road is immense.

KEY TAKEAWAYS

- It's essential to know *who* you are talking to. When it comes to messaging, one size doesn't fit all.

- Make plans for different buyers as they pass through the five stages of the buying cycle for considered purchases:
  - Inquire
  - Learn
  - Evaluate
  - Justify
  - Select

- A persona profiles a stakeholder's specific role in the buying process and has the following components:
  - Profile overview
  - Pain points
  - Key drivers/motivators
  - Role in the buying committee
  - Effective influences

- Content-Development Tips
  - Make a one-to-one connection.
  - Start with "Why?"
  - Use a personal tone.

- Operationalize the Personas
  - Learn to read *digital body language*—the mousetrails of data generated by site visitors.
  - Correlate the activities of your 10 most recent customers with their site behavior and buying process.
  - Identify the unique combination of fields in your database that correspond to the characteristics of your defined buyer personas.
  - Use inferred data to flesh out personas.

©2012 DemandGen International, Inc.

Chapter 4

---◆---

THE DEMAND FUNNEL: THE PATHWAY TO REVENUE

When I was at Ellie Mae, we launched a demand-generation campaign that I thought was pretty darn successful. We had hundreds of people filling out forms and requesting free trials. When we hit 1,000 leads, brimming with confidence, I strolled over to Joe in sales and, with as much false modesty and casualness as I could muster, asked, "So, hey, what do you think of all these leads we've generated?"

"David, let me put this to you simply: Your leads suck."

I imagine I must have given it the old cartoon head-shake double-take. What? We were *cranking* out the leads. How could he have a problem? Well, it turns out his problem with our performance was legit. We were generating lots of inquiries from loan processors. Yes, they can influence a sale—but the sales folks don't want to spend much time with them because they aren't the decision makers. It's the mortgage brokers who make the software-procurement decisions for their business. They were the "king salmon" that sales was looking to land. By contrast, we were capturing little more than large schools of minnows in our nets.

Virtually every marketer has heard the complaint—in any variety of G, PG-13, or R-rated versions: The quality of the sales leads simply doesn't measure up to the sales team's expectations. The sales team considers a lead to be someone who's ready to talk to them *now* and who can approve and fund the purchase. Marketing, however, has often fallen into the trap of using the term "lead" to mean anyone who's responded in any way to a lead generation campaign.

I know that, early in my career, I considered any "hand-raiser" to be a lead. But, like Joe, my counterparts in sales viewed a lead only as a prospective buyer who was ready to buy from the right person, right now.

So, the first step in improving alignment between sales and marketing—in creating a Lead Management system (an umbrella term encompassing the set of *integrated,* unified processes and systems for funneling prospects through a process with scoring and nurturing)—is to find a common vocabulary and glossary of terms that each group can agree upon.

Just this first milestone alone will go a long way in helping us reduce what has been inevitable friction and create a systematic and structured framework—*Demand Funnel*—for categorizing prospective customers. Defining the Demand Funnel is an important early step in the alignment of sales and marketing, and, as such, *must* be a collaborative process between the two camps.

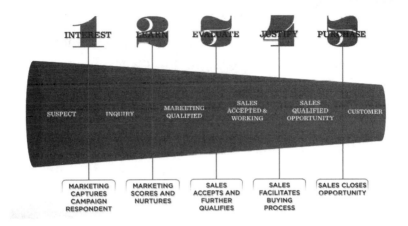

INTEGRATED SALES & MARKETING FUNNEL
KEY STAGES OF THE B2B BUYING PROCESS

WHAT IS A LEAD?

Can we agree on something right here and now? Let's STOP calling something a "lead" if it isn't a lead! In fact, we could eliminate the use of the standalone word "lead" entirely. Every time we use the word "lead" it should come with a qualifier: a marketing qualified lead, a sales accepted lead (we'll explain those terms shortly).

I have a favorite question I like to ask audiences at my seminars and workshops, one that is deceptively simple: "What is a lead?" Can't be that hard to answer, right? Well, I've had the privilege of asking that question to thousands of people in venues around the world—and the answers are *never* alike. The definitions vary—sometimes significantly—and those differences are revealing. We need to bridge those differences and create a common understanding.

CREATING THE TAXONOMY OF LEAD MANAGEMENT

The Demand Funnel is both a language and a process model for how leads move from inquiry to customer. Defining its stages gives you the foundation for segmentation, scoring, routing, nurturing, and reporting and creates that common language between sales and marketing.

But note: Simply creating the stages and declaring "we have a funnel" is nowhere near enough. We need to conduct a detailed exercise to clearly assign meaning, ownership, and process to each stage of the funnel and fully adopting the new Demand Funnel as the foundation for generating demand and following through on it.

Think about the shape of the funnel. Typically, the *narrowest* part, the bottom, has the entire sales staff assigned to it. But the *widest* part—where all the prospects enter—is the responsibility of far fewer marketing people. As marketers, our job is to generate a lot of responses to fill that funnel and make the top as wide as possible. But as the shape suggests, fewer and fewer will move down each stage, which is why we need a well-defined system—underpinned by a factory mentality and sophisticated marketing automation—to make that happen efficiently and effectively. An effective Demand Funnel includes:

- Agreed-upon stage definitions and a taxonomy
- Defined stage ownership and triggers for conversion between stages
- Service level agreements (SLAs) for each stage
- Marketing automation and customer relationship management systems to support the funnel model and processes
- Forecasts and measurements for the quantities of each stage and the conversion percentages between stages

A USEFUL TAXONOMY FROM SIRIUS DECISIONS

The original Demand Waterfall introduced by SiriusDecisions offers us a very useful framework for thinking about a standard, serviceable Demand Funnel, and I can heartily recommend it as a starting point for a taxonomy in your organization.

- **Suspect**—An unidentified potential buyer in the total available market for the product or service.

- **Inquiry**—A raw response or hand-raiser. Relatively little is known about the prospect at this point.

- **Marketing-Qualified Lead**—An inquiry that meets minimum fit criteria (qualification and interest) as jointly defined by sales and marketing and is ready for sales engagement.

- **Sales-Accepted Lead**—A lead that has been formally accepted by sales, which must work the lead within a given timeframe to determine if a qualified opportunity exists.

- **Sales-Qualified Lead**—Sales has confirmed that a viable opportunity exists and has committed it to the pipeline with an estimated dollar value and timeframe to close.

- **Customer**—An opportunity that has come to fruition.

This initial taxonomy is great starting point for B2B organizations, but don't feel you must force fit your process into these defined stages and terms. You may have to incorporate teleprospecting into your stages, and you may want to drop the word "lead" altogether from the stage names. You certainly can and should consider customizing or expanding this taxonomy to comfortably align with and support your specific sales and marketing process. That said, too many stages and non-intuitive definitions might suggest an overly complicated process that will undoubtedly make adoption and reporting more difficult.

OPERATIONALIZE THE TAXONOMY

Next, we must take the agreed-upon taxonomy from the whiteboard and populate it into our marketing automation and CRM systems. That means setting up actual fields in those applications and the workflow to move prospects through the funnel. What makes a lead sales-ready? What's the difference between an inquiry and an MQL *in your business*? When should marketing hand off a lead to sales? What are the criteria for defining when a lead has matured enough to enter the next phase of the funnel? These are some of the questions we must answer to transition from the theoretical discussions to actual praxis.

I know first-hand that very few companies have the strategic and technical experience to implement this framework. The companies that have been most successful leverage outside firms (like my company, DemandGen) to facilitate the process and implement it. That's not supposed to sound like a selfish plug. I simply envision you probably asking yourself right now, "OK, David, who the heck in my firm would know how to do this?" and the answer is "Probably no one." OK, maybe it's a plug.

You may have noticed that the stages so far account for prospects moving down the funnel toward the ultimate one: Customer. But what do we do about those who are not yet ready to buy?

BELIEVE IN RECYCLING

Naturally, not every lead flows neatly through the Demand Funnel in an orderly way. Some leads stubbornly remain in early stages of the Demand Funnel. In fact, in most cases, fewer than 10 percent of inquiries will result in closed/won business. To address those stuck leads, we must expand the Demand Funnel to include a couple of additional stages that happen *outside* the funnel.

- **Recycling**—The handoff to sales takes place, but the prospect doesn't respond or doesn't have a budget, or some other roadblock crops up somewhere down the funnel. Nonetheless, sales thinks this prospect still may have potential in the future. The prospect status is set to "Recycled," placing it back into the funnel for further nurturing with the goal of reengagement at a later time.

- **Disqualified**—If the inquiry name is something like "Mickey Mouse" from GetLost.com, we can safely assume that it will never develop into any sort of opportunity. We should disqualify it to prevent it from being any further distraction to our sales or marketing efforts.

The power of the Demand Funnel not only comes from creating a common language for sales and marketing, it also stems from the ability to measure volume and velocity toward the end of the pipeline. Following the manufacturing analogy, the Demand Funnel lets you measure raw materials (inquiries), work in progress (qualified leads), waste (disqualified leads), and output (customers). Your vice president of sales will be a hero when he can confidently report the pipeline status, because he will know the conversion metrics down the funnel and the volume in each stage.

We'll get into analytics later—in Chapter 7. But for now, the key performance indicators of our Demand Funnel will track how many leads are in each stage. What percentage convert from stage to stage? How long does each conversion take, on average? What are the high and low outliers? The goal is to clearly see the *quantity*, *velocity*, and *predictability* of closed/won sales from higher stages of the funnel where marketing is generating volumes of inquiries and marketing qualified leads.

MANUFACTURING DEMAND IN ACTION

visionapp

As an active player in the cloud computing market for more than a decade, visionapp supplies software and services for private, public, and hybrid cloud solutions. Having deployed a marketing automation system, visionapp was eager to set up a comprehensive automated event invitation and registration process for its CloudFactory roadshow, an event for professionals exploring the emerging trend of cloud computing.

"We felt that our marketing automation system could benefit visionapp in several ways," said Marina Walser, chief marketing officer. "We wanted to enhance our ability to track and measure the CloudFactory campaign's effectiveness, and improve event attendance."

The Secret Recipe: Infrastructure, Integration, and Tracking

First, the team ran a data audit to assess its prospect profiles—were they complete and did they use appropriate levels of standardization? Next, the database was segmented based on gender, language, and other event-specific criteria, then standardized to allow better targeting. Next, the team designed the program flow and integration with external portals and Web pages. Data needed to flow seamlessly from one system to another to provide a better customer experience from the first click to the actual registration.

Finally, the program leveraged a prospect's digital footprint by tracking activity and interactions. This drove up registrations by creating a relevant dialogue, because the program was tailored to match a prospect's online behavior and engagement level. Each communication was highly customized, event-triggered, and delivered real-time.

The Numbers Tell a Story of Success

The results have been excellent for visionapp. The company reported a higher email open rate that it attributes to the relevancy, timing, personalization, and segmentation applied. Open rates were up to 20 percent for inactive contacts and 47 percent for active and engaged prospects. In addition, visionapp saw an increase in the clickthrough rate when targeting active contacts.

While these metrics prove that automated, well-designed programs have a significant impact on soft metrics, ultimately visionapp's goal was to drive registration. The result there was very impressive: Registrations increased from 5–10 per show to 90 per show—an increase of as much as 1,700 percent.

MANUFACTURING DEMAND IN ACTION
e.Republic

When e.Republic, Inc.—a leading publishing, research, event, and new media company—decided to implement marketing automation, the requirements were particularly complex. e.Republic offers several controlled-circulation publications to select targeted audiences. Each year, it sends out 25 million emails to a database of more than a quarter of a million people. To maintain its certification from BPA Worldwide, which provides independent assurance to advertisers that a publication's data tracking processes and systems are accurate, e.Republic must meet stringent requirements.

"BPA rules prevent us from having one form for subscribing to multiple publications, so we collect a *lot* of data," says Drew Noel, e.Republic's Corporate Marketing Director. "We needed to manage subscription data from all our various publications, which have many custom aspects."

Because of the sophisticated nature of e.Republic's email marketing needs, the company implemented a popular marketing automation system for lead scoring and nurturing. After an intensive training and implementation cycle, the company has achieved significant gains—particularly in marketing operations, where the company has saved time and achieved greater accuracy.

- **Analyzing Relationships**—e.Republic was able to quickly "cookie" a significant portion of its database, connecting all of its key contacts in the CRM system, to analyze the depth of Web visits, see what actions visitors are taking, and uncover relationships between online and offline content. "We had really no way to do that before," said Noel. Overall, ***open rates have increased by 17 percent and effectiveness has increased by 22 percent.***

- **Campaign Speed**—The system has cut campaign execution time from weeks to hours or minutes. "Before, emails had to be created almost from scratch every time. Now we can repurpose emails in minutes," Noel said. "The IT department used to be involved in creating a single Web landing page, which took about two weeks for turnaround. Now a marketing staffer can do it in an hour."

- **Accurate Reporting**—On the reporting side, e.Republic has much greater accuracy, as well as a broader range of reporting options. "We became very familiar with the reporting interface and the vast amount of metrics available," said Noel.

- **A Clearer Picture**—e.Republic produces more than 150 events annually and is using its MA tool for event registration. "All our registrations integrate with the CRM system, so we have a full picture of all our event attendees, and a fully unified database that is very clean."

Using Marketing Data to Create Dynamic Editorial

e.Republic's future plans include applying the principles of lead scoring to all audiences. "We've learned that implicit (behavior-based) data is much more accurate in telling us what content a consumer really wants than explicit data (what they have told us)," Noel explained. "So we want to only push out the stories that a reader is interested in, cut email traffic, and maintain or increase website traffic."

KEY TAKEAWAYS

- A Demand Funnel is a conceptual framework—based on agreement between sales and marketing—for tracking leads as they proceed through the buying cycle.

- The Demand Funnel includes:
  - Agreed-upon stage definitions and a taxonomy
  - Defined stage-ownership and triggers for conversion between stages
  - Service level agreements (SLAs) for each stage
  - Marketing automation and customer relationship management (CRM) systems to support the funnel model and processes
  - Forecasts and measurements for the quantities of each stage and the conversion percentage between stages.

- The SiriusDecisions "Demand Waterfall" Taxonomy is a great starting point:
  - Suspect
  - Inquiry
  - Marketing-Qualified Lead
  - Sales-Accepted Lead
  - Sales-Qualified Lead
  - Customer

- Believe in Recycling—Sometimes good leads just aren't ready yet. Don't throw them out.

- Understand the volume and velocity of your Demand Funnel.

Chapter 5

LEAD SCORING DEMYSTIFIED

Now that we've created a Demand Funnel taxonomy, we need an automated way to distinguish between an inquiry and a MQL, using the criteria that have been collaboratively defined by sales and marketing, and to prioritize/rank all leads so that sales focuses on the best ones, as measured by qualification and interest.

That's where lead scoring enters the picture. Lead scoring is the process of assigning a ranking to sales prospects based on an understanding of the prospects' interests and buying intentions. If you don't have a lead scoring system, you're missing out on one of the biggest payoffs of marketing automation. Simply put, there is no better way to measure the quality of your leads *and* improve the effectiveness of your sales team in a scalable manner.

What characteristics are common to leads that merit an A-level rating? What about B or C ratings? What online behaviors best define a prospect's interest?

Although most lead scoring systems use some type of algorithm as part of the ranking process, lead scoring isn't just a formulaic calculation. Today, we can leverage the ability to track and interpret the prospect's online behavior and link that behavior to different stages of the buying cycle. With those critical insights, we can better interpret that behavior and use our knowledge to dramatically improve conversion rates and sales efficiency.

It's also important to clearly understand what lead scoring is *not*. It's *not* a predictor of who will close or who will buy. It's *not* a forecast. Rather, it provides a prioritized, inbound to-do list for the sales rep and a way to systematically status leads from inquiry to marketing qualified.

Having consulted on countless lead scoring models for clients over the years, I can tell you that almost no two lead scoring systems use the same criteria to score and rank a lead (unless they sell the same product to the same customer). That's because the qualification criteria are typically different between any two companies. That said, there are four common lead scoring models used today.

- **Interest-Only Scoring**—Here, we use only behavior to gauge a prospect's interest and suitability.

- **Qualification-Only Scoring**—Conversely, in this model, we ignore behavior and focus solely on "fit"—the characteristics/attributes of the prospect.

- **Two-Dimensional Scoring**—Here, we're combining both fit criteria and behavior in a single model.

- **Predictive Lead Scoring**—This emerging model essentially looks at historical data to determine patterns of won business, and compares new prospects to the pattern to establish a likelihood of purchase.

Whichever model you choose, you still must decide how you will approach the actual mathematical scoring of each lead.

In the *cumulative* method, you assign points to each interest behavior and fitness attribute criteria and aggregate the points to derive a total score. Although this method can sometimes lead to false positives or false negatives, it's the easiest way to build a lead scoring model.

Scoring Matrix

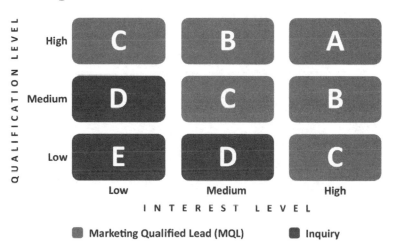

Figure 5.1 Two-Dimensional Lead Scoring Matrix

The *dimensional* method calculates the lead score using the intersection of two dimensions: the interest score and the qualification score. Rather than add them together to produce a score, you create a multi-quadrant grid (see Figure 5.1 above). The place on the grid where these two scores intersect is the lead rating. I find this two-dimensional model is the most reliable and flexible so I'll focus on it to demystify lead scoring for you. Let's start with some definitions and then discuss the process for coming up with your own lead scoring system.

QUALIFICATION AND INTEREST: THE TWO DIMENSIONS OF SCORING

In this model, a prospect's lead score is determined by collecting data on two dimensions: qualification level and interest level. (Others have called this "Fit vs. Interest" or "Profile vs. Engagement"—the principles are nearly identical.) We use that data in an algorithm to calculate a score. Two classes of information play into the data we need for proper dimensional lead scoring: explicit and implicit.

- **Explicit** attributes are provided by the prospect, such as company size, industry, role, product/service interests, and more. Explicit attributes are typically obtained through website forms when a lead first comes into the system. For instance, when a site visitor tours your site, you might only measure behavior you'll use later. But if the prospect requests downloadable content, such as a white paper, or access to a demo or free trial, you use this "give-to-get" opportunity to ask for more information and present a form with two to four qualification fields. The marketing automation system uses the data from these fields to assign points and give you an explicit score—more commonly called a qualification score.

- **Implicit** attributes are based on online behaviors, the digital body language we discussed earlier. These behaviors are used to calculate the interest score. Examples might include visiting a website (frequency and recency are the important characteristics here), clicking through emails, registering for webinars, completing certain forms, and even viewing particular areas of the website that can indicate buyer interest—and their stage in the buying cycle.

ESTABLISH THE TASK FORCE

When we start to build a lead scoring model—that is, as we start to define the explicit and implicit attributes that define qualification and interest—the first step is sometimes the hardest: We must get sales and marketing in the same room for several hours, and establish a new common language around lead taxonomy. I suggest you pull together the key stakeholders in sales and marketing and make sure you've tapped experienced, in-the-trenches resources from both teams for the project to decide what factors make a lead qualified—this is not the time to train your entry-level staff who lack the experience in deciding what factors make a lead qualified.

Make sure you have executive support to ensure this effort is made a high priority for sales and marketing. Also, consider bringing in an expert resource to help guide your project. Trust me, it can save you a lot of time and pain. A neutral third party can be very helpful in mediating disagreements between strong-minded colleagues. Here are some other "taskforce pitfalls" to avoid:

- Commit the appropriate amount of time to the process. Don't allow the team to make hasty decisions in a one-hour meeting—it's too important.

- Don't let any one person or group dominate the discussion, "bully" the process, or insist that marketing ask inappropriate form questions in your qualification model (including such painful evergreens as, "Do you have a budget? What's your purchase timeframe?"). The likelihood of you getting valuable answers is low. Unless you can "disguise" these questions, you'll get lots of forms-abandonment or falsified info. Asking "Do you have budget?" is like asking "How much money do you make?" on a first date: tacky and inappropriate.

- Don't fall for claims that implementing lead scoring can be "quick and easy." Many marketing automation vendors make this process seem a little too easy. The reality is that it's *essential* for your lead-scoring model to use business-specific qualification criteria that have been well vetted by sales and marketing, can be integrated with your CRM system, and are supported by sales training to ensure proper adoption. Those are essential steps that many marketing automation vendors would be happier to rush through or skip altogether. However, the best lead-scoring formula in the world won't deliver the efficiencies and increased conversions you want if it's not properly set up and implemented. Rush it, and you'll simply accelerate bad processes and incomplete thinking.

- Prepare well. Insufficient preparation before the lead-qualification meeting can sabotage your efforts. Ask your task force—well before the meeting—to carefully think about what they believe truly qualifies someone as a meaningful lead. Ask your sales folks to start taking notes to capture the questions that they're asking on the phone (or in person). Explain that you're not looking for BANT—you want the true dimensions and characteristics of the ideal customer profile. This is hard in most cases, but the rewards of getting it right are huge.

YOUR IDEAL CUSTOMER: THE QUALIFICATION MODEL

One way to build your qualification model is through a *subjective* analysis that's informed by the judgment and experience of your task force. Ask your salespeople to describe the ideal customer. What are the attributes that make up the total profile? Marketing folks should be able to articulate the "matchmaking" process and describe what a Marketing Qualified Lead looks like. Members from both teams must be able to explain their reasoning so it can be clearly understood. Statistics and examples can be helpful, but truly understanding each other's beliefs is the purpose of this exercise.

Discuss the qualification of a sales lead until you reach a consensus. In some organizations, this will be easy; in others, it may be painful. Either way, it's critical! Once the qualification criteria have been determined, update your forms on the website to capture that information from your prospects.

Of course, some data-rich companies are interested in *objective* models for lead qualification—in other words, predictive scoring that is calculated using historical data. They carefully sift through and analyze mountains of historical data to determine what patterns indicate qualification and interest. For instance, an elaborate model might analyze closed/won accounts to find the patterns that indicate a good buyer. This is traditionally a time-consuming and costly method, but it can be very effective. New tools are just being introduced, though, that promise to ease the process of forming a predictive lead-scoring model. At the time of publishing, there have not been enough success stories for me to recommend or caution you away from these systems, but it's worth noting that there may be other options available. Many qualification models actually blend components of both subjective and objective techniques.

MANUFACTURING DEMAND IN ACTION

Bella Pictures

Bella Pictures is a technology-driven leader in the $4 billion market for wedding photography services. Although planning a wedding can take up to a year or more, the photography decision process usually happens within a very brief two- to three-week period. Much like getting the perfect shot of the bride and groom, converting a lead to a sale means picking exactly the right moment.

Bella's business model calls for an inside sales team to set appointments at just the right time and enable the outside sales staff to meet with the couple to understand their photography style and accelerate the sales process. Unfortunately, Bella's early approaches to lead scoring were very static, based solely on qualification attributes from a Web inquiry form. Although the score could range from 1-100, most leads were clustered at about 45 and this vagueness translated into a diminished ability to prioritize leads and predict monthly goals.

"We wanted a lead-scoring program that included qualification *and* interest information, which was a new concept for us," said Teresa Almaraz, channel marketing manager. "We learned we could dynamically score leads as they come in. We could look at both qualification attributes *and* the interest attributes. For example, a person may be qualified to look like a lead worth contacting according to what she selected on the website form, but if she is not spending time on the website, she's not opening our emails, or she's unsubscribing, she's probably not the person we want our inside sales team to spend time calling."

Focusing on Facts Delivers Results

With a consultant, Bella built profiles based on behavioral and buying data to gain a true picture of where prospects were in the buying cycle. Significant attributes—both positive and negative variables—were measured using statistics to measure relative strength of qualification and interest. The analysis of historical data helped Bella identify a single specific question that qualified prospects: "Have you selected a venue?" Using these findings, a scoring algorithm that combined fit and interest was developed.

"It's incredible how well this lead-scoring program has worked for us," says Almaraz. "The dynamic lead scoring program accounts for both qualification and interest variables, so the range of scores has expanded. We see a nice distribution of scores from 1 to 100, rather than everyone being 45, so we know that these values mean something."

Leads are continuously evaluated and scored, so each time the inside sales person reviews the list, a prospect's score may update. Interest activity—such as website visits, email clickthroughs, unsubscribes, bouncebacks, and more—trigger revised scores, so that inside sales continually sees the hottest leads at the top of the call list.

Today, Bella Pictures predicts appointment set-rates using lead scores, which has helped the company forecast its end-of-month conversions more accurately. "For example, we know that if we bring in a certain number of 80s, we will get a specific number of appointments from them. We know how well 60s and 70s do in terms of conversion. Inside sales has become more efficient because it now takes fewer calls to make the same number of appointments. This has really been huge for us."

Qualification "Dos and Don'ts"

DO	DON'T
✔ DO create an internal Demand Generation Task Force between marketing and sales to reach agreement on common lead definitions, descriptions, and action points.	✘ DON'T use overly simplistic progressive numeric scoring methods that often return false positive leads because of high interest scores.
✔ DO use marketing automation and CRM technology, and get lead scoring systems up and running right. If lead scoring isn't a core expertise, engage a lead scoring expert to guide your efforts, provide best-practice experience, and eliminate guesswork.	✘ DON'T build a model based on BANT criteria for determining fit. Asking budget and timeframe questions on forms is not best practice. It's a turn-off.
✔ DO cross-reference demographics and firmagraphics against individual lead scores to create buyer profiles that provide better predictability.	✘ DON'T use qualification criteria for verticals or markets where you don't currently have ideal prospect matches. Fit criteria should be based on your current ideal customer profile.

DO	DON'T
✔ DO weigh and track only as many variables as needed to generate ideal leads that meet your qualification criteria (as described above). If you track too many variables, you will unnecessarily complicate the model. You're not building a system for finding sales' soul mate. You just want to prioritize qualified leads for sales.	✘ DON'T go it alone. Automated lead scoring has a lot of moving parts—lead definitions, asset weighting, behavioral targeting—so even large enterprises bring in experts to set them up and prove the model. Change management is a big factor in successful adoption, and that may require an outside "agent of change."
✔ DO engage prospects with fresh content that's appropriate for specific buyers and phases.	✘ DON'T forget to factor in digital body language to establish behavioral attributes.

YOUR IDEAL CUSTOMER: THE INTEREST MODEL

Interest is the other dimension of lead scoring. Someone may meet the *qualifications* established for a lead, but if they don't show any buyer interest, the lead score is lower. Remember, interest is derived from implicit data by reading the digital body language of the prospect. It should incorporate the various online activities of prospect engagement and possibly others:

- Website behavior such as forms submission and download activity
- Email responsiveness—do they click through your messages to landing pages?
- Online-event registration

- Content downloads and sign-ups for free trials or demos

- Recency and frequency of these activities

"Reverse engineering" a selection of customer wins to uncover common behavior patterns of buyers can be effective in selecting behaviors on which to score. But quite often, people are simply guessing when they decide how many points to give for each type of interest behavior. That's understandable since few firms have experience developing lead-scoring systems, but if you're going to go it alone and not seek outside consultation, test the results of your model in a pilot with sales before you launch it broadly.

Two-Dimensional Scoring at a Glance

- Identify two to four qualitative criteria to measure qualification.

- Identify the online behaviors that correlate with prospect interest.

- Use both measurements to set a rating for each new prospect.

- Ensure that an effective scoring hand-off process exists between sales and marketing.

- Create a simple and effective way to show the scored leads in your CRM.

- Gather at least one quarter's worth of scoring data and analyze scoring distribution through to closed/won opportunities.

- Implement a qualitative feedback loop with sales to refine the model.

MAKING THE GRADE: THE RATING SYSTEM

Once we have the qualification and interest model, we must develop a scoring formula that combines these two dimensions into a very simple rating system. First, we assign weights to each of the qualification and interest metrics we've previously defined. Is recency super-important? Then give it added weight. Is the downloading of particular buyer-centric content a key signal? Then give it added weight.

What about cumulative score? In other words, how long should a prospect's behavior matter? If she downloaded a white paper three months ago—and did nothing afterward—her score should decay a bit to indicate that lack of interest. But be careful not to reduce the interest score *too* much due to a lack of recent activity, since buyers often show heavy website activity for a period and then rely less on the website because they have already consumed the content available. In other words—"once highly interested, always interested."

Unless you have nurturing programs to maintain interest (which we will cover in Chapter 6), lead scores will almost always peak in advance of a purchase transaction. It's better to show the peak score to sales, instead of systematically degrading the score because of inactivity. Why? The sales person might not realize that these are "automatic score reductions" and might opt not to engage with a lead who *seems* to be showing declining interest.

Now that we have our qualification and interest scores, we're ready to create an overall lead rating. The goal here is to **take the complexity out** of this process. In my experience, a simple A-E grid provides an excellent solution.

Scoring Matrix

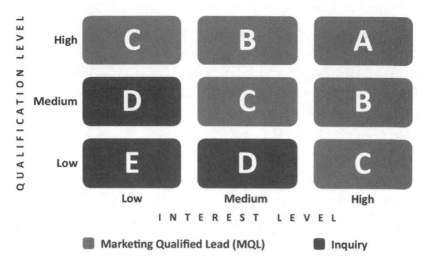

With the above lead-scoring matrix, we can establish a default definition that an A, B, or C lead is a marketing-qualified lead (MQL) while D and E leads are merely inquiries (in our Demand Funnel).

The best way to present lead scores to the sales team in your CRM system is to use a highly visual metaphor that requires virtually no training to understand and adopt. What you want is an "at-a-glance" knowledge of the top prospects. Ask yourself these questions:

- Can the rep easily find the lead rating in the screen being presented?
- Can the rep determine instantly (say, two seconds) that a specific lead is worth contacting?
- Can the rep instantly see how qualified the lead is?
- Can the rep instantly see how interested the lead is?

The point here is that presenting a numerical score in a field (62 out of 100, 33 percent) won't achieve the simple at-a-glance recognition we're seeking that makes lead scoring effective for the salesperson. Whether you choose stars, hot peppers, flames, or some other meaningful graphic, a visual rating is the best way we've found to present the overall lead score, followed by thermometer-style meters or icons that indicate qualification and interest level.

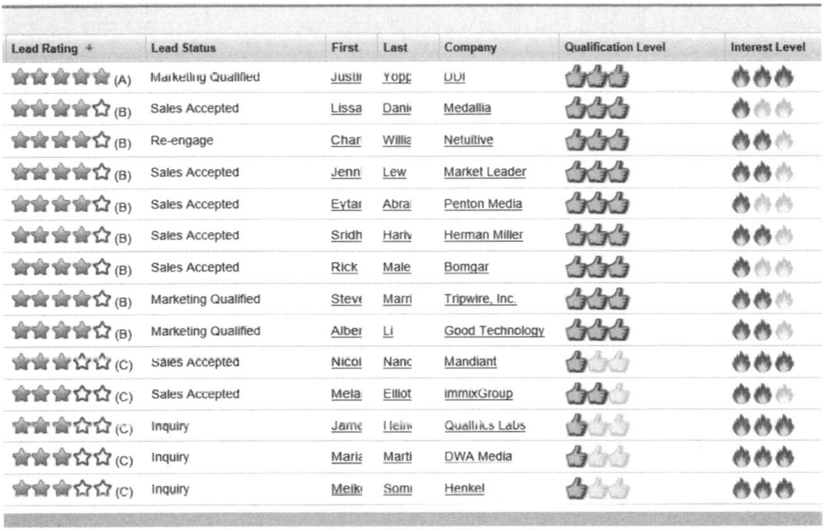

Lead Rating ↓	Lead Status	First	Last	Company	Qualification Level	Interest Level
★★★★★ (A)	Marketing Qualified	Justin	Yopp	DDI	👍👍👍	🔥🔥🔥
★★★★☆ (B)	Sales Accepted	Lissa	Dani	Medallia	👍👍👍	🔥🔥🔥
★★★★☆ (B)	Re-engage	Char	Willia	Netuitive	👍👍👍	🔥🔥🔥
★★★★☆ (B)	Sales Accepted	Jenn	Lew	Market Leader	👍👍👍	🔥🔥🔥
★★★★☆ (B)	Sales Accepted	Eytar	Abra	Penton Media	👍👍👍	🔥🔥🔥
★★★★☆ (B)	Sales Accepted	Sridh	Harl	Herman Miller	👍👍👍	🔥🔥🔥
★★★★☆ (B)	Sales Accepted	Rick	Male	Bomgar	👍👍👍	🔥🔥🔥
★★★★☆ (B)	Marketing Qualified	Steve	Marri	Tripwire, Inc.	👍👍👍	🔥🔥🔥
★★★★☆ (B)	Marketing Qualified	Alber	Li	Good Technology	👍👍👍	🔥🔥🔥
★★★☆☆ (C)	Sales Accepted	Nicol	Nanc	Mandiant	👍👍👍	🔥🔥🔥
★★★☆☆ (C)	Sales Accepted	Mela	Elliot	immixGroup	👍👍👍	🔥🔥🔥
★★★☆☆ (C)	Inquiry	Jame	Heln	Qualtrics Labs	👍👍👍	🔥🔥🔥
★★★☆☆ (C)	Inquiry	Maria	Marti	DWA Media	👍👍👍	🔥🔥🔥
★★★☆☆ (C)	Inquiry	Meik	Som	Henkel	👍👍👍	🔥🔥🔥

Figure 5.2 Example of an effective lead scoring layout for sales.

Finally, we need one additional level of collaboration on the project. We need to agree on what each party will *do* with a qualified lead. In other words, we need a service level agreement (SLA) between sales and marketing that clearly establishes the actions and timeframes for each participant. For instance, when a prospective buyer becomes a marketing qualified lead (MQL) and that designation changes in the CRM system, the assigned sales rep may have an SLA to attempt contact within 24 hours. Or there can be SLAs governing the method of contact and the frequency ("cadence") of sales contact over a given time period—such as an agreement to email every 72 hours for two weeks. Marketing's SLA might specify the type of follow-up communication and "snooze" period for recycled leads when there's no response to sales by the prospect after an agreed number of attempts.

These shared expectations documented in SLAs help the sales and marketing organization move forward in an organized fashion. All tasks and timeframes are defined and agreed to—and that helps prevent misunderstandings and "dropped balls."

As you'll see in the sidebar below from the Demand Gen Report, an e-media publication covering B2B marketing, the best practices for lead scoring aren't necessarily known or being practiced. (Note: Demand Gen Report is not affiliated with my firm, DemandGen International)

Tremendous Opportunity Remains for Lead Scoring

- Only 32 percent said they were "effectively using" lead scoring.

- 3 in 10 respondents said they were using scoring "somewhat."

- 39 percent were not using lead scoring tools at all.

- Source: Demand Gen Report

TECHNOLOGY IMPLEMENTATION "DOS AND DON'TS"

DO	DON'T
✔ DO seek the advice of an experienced lead scoring expert to help you develop your model and be an agent of change.	✘ DON'T sabotage the nurturing process (which feeds the sales lead queue) by skimping on content. Great B2B content is scored on how its granularity and complexity match buyer's needs.
✔ DO use lead scoring to track online behavior—aka digital body language—enabling you to follow along as prospects consume content and emit important buying signals that trigger sales action.	✘ DON'T botch the balancing act of only using qualification criteria. Online dating sites might use 29 criteria to find your soul mate, but B2B lead scoring should also factor in buyer behavior.
✔DO make sure that lead scores calculated in the marketing automation system are visually presented in the CRM system so that sales reps know exactly who to contact, and how best to approach them.	✘ DON'T expect immediate impact. Allow at least two to three months for your implementation to start showing measurable results. New lead scoring algorithms must be analyzed and refined using sufficient data collection.

MAINTAINING YOUR LEAD-SCORING SYSTEM

A lead-scoring framework is not a "set-it-and-forget-it" proposition. There are several ongoing tasks you need to manage to ensure your model stays abreast of your business's changing positions and goals. One way is right at launch time: Consider starting with just a smaller subset of sales reps who can give anecdotal feedback that has high value.

First, periodically review the SLAs that have been established between sales and marketing. Are they still feasible? Are they still being followed? What are the statistics on SLA "violations" (e.g. more than 48 hours passing before an MQL gets a call from sales)? Do the stats show a need for revisiting the SLAs, a need for sales training, or a need for greater staffing/coverage?

Always keep a channel open to obtain feedback from your teammates in sales. They are closer to the customers and can be your early-warning system for detecting and responding to changes in the market. Set up a reporting dashboard to see the aggregate distribution of lead scores—how many A's, B's, and C's—and gauge how effective the scoring has been.

Create reporting dashboards to present concise summaries of key performance indicators (KPIs). These can give you earlier indications of areas where improvements are needed. For example, you'll definitely want to track your opportunity-to-close ratios to gauge the effectiveness of your scoring system. If your ratio is low, it may indicate two important changes are needed:

- **Reexamine Your Qualification Questions**—Over time, the effectiveness of your qualification questions can fade as market imperatives and business priorities shift and evolve. Be sure to continually review the criteria for qualification and the questions you ask your prospects to keep them meaningful and relevant to your scoring system.

- **Reexamine Your Weightings**—Similarly, it can be helpful to review the weightings that are assigned to different qualification and interest factors and metrics. For example, perhaps recency isn't quite as important as it used to be in indicating interest level. Look at recent sales wins and identify shifts in buyer behavior—then, factor those into your scoring model.

Try to find your false positives and false negatives and see how you can turn these lapses into model improvements.

HOW DO YOU KNOW IF LEAD SCORING IS PAYING OFF? CALCULATING ROI

If there's one thing that is common to marketing managers everywhere, it's the continual need to justify your spending—but, of course, the benefits of marketing are notoriously hard to measure. The good news: lead scoring is one of the easiest marketing programs to justify with two key measurement opportunities:

GREATER SALES EFFICIENCY

This quantitative metric is best measured over time, but a little qualitative research within the first 30 days of launch will let you know if you're on the right track. Interview your top salespeople who use the lead-scoring system regularly. Get their candid feedback about whether they're finding A and B leads more responsive to their attempts to engage. The answer should be yes! If not, your demand generation team may need to revisit the scoring model.

To measure sales efficiency quantitatively, track the time from when a lead record is first accepted by sales (meaning it's being worked) to the time when an opportunity is created in the CRM. Plot this measurement for some period prior to the launch of lead scoring so that you have a baseline for comparison. As more salespeople adopt the system, you should see a progressive shortening of the timeframe from acceptance to opportunity creation.

HIGHER CONVERSION TO OPPORTUNITY

To see if you're increasing conversions per rep, look at the number of opportunities that the rep typically creates in a given period of time. (Again, it's a good idea to track this data for benchmark purposes prior to the lead-scoring system deployment.) If your top rep normally created 15 opportunities and, after the implementation of lead scoring, that number jumps to 25, it might seem obvious that you are seeing improvement. But it's not quite that simple. Here's why:

- **The 80-20 Rule**—First, most sales organizations have a few individuals who skew the numbers. The 80-20 rule typically applies: 80 percent of the opportunities are created by 20 percent of the sales team. You may find that a small number of reps generate a lot of the opportunities.

So initially, take an average of total opportunities created by the entire sales team per month. This approach gives you a general perspective of how your new model is working. But when you have at least three months of behavioral data, delve down and look at the numbers for each rep.

- **Adoption Challenges**—Most likely, lead scoring will not be immediately and fully adopted by every one of your sales reps. Some folks will completely ignore you and your newfangled process for prioritizing leads. You can have the world's best lead-scoring system—but without adoption and utilization, you won't see the benefits in sales efficiency. Expect to see remarkable improvements in efficiency by a small number of reps who are embracing it, and no change in the efficiency of others who may not be fully convinced of its value. (Showing this data as a graph to the team may spur some enthusiasm—and healthy competition.)

- **Sometimes Less Is More**—Maybe your numbers look quite different. Instead of 15 opportunities, suddenly your top rep is only averaging nine per month. If you see a drop in the number of opportunities created, don't panic and rush down to unplug the system. You've probably uncovered a dirty little secret: Your opportunity-creation process was a bit loose, meaning it allowed reps to create many sub-par opportunities. A short-term drop in absolute numbers of opportunities isn't a matter for concern. The endgame is whether sales converts more opportunities into won business.

Don't be surprised to find that the number of created opportunities goes down, but the number converted to wins goes up. Measure on percentage of closed/won business to the opportunities created. If that top rep is now closing 75 percent rather than 50 percent, that's the kind of statistic that really matters. It's a sign that your folks are spending their time on the right stuff: working fewer opportunities, but doing a better job on the ones they work. And that's a good definition of "sales efficiency."

WE CAN ALL JUST GET ALONG!

Don't forget, when you're looking at ROI, to consider the intangible benefits of building and using lead scoring. A less quantitative way to measure its impact on your organization is to see how it enhances and strengthens the relationship between sales and marketing. Most companies find that their conversations are more positive and constructive, with less accusation and assigning of blame. There's typically a much greater emphasis on team orientation that extends far beyond the lead-scoring project itself. To my mind, that's almost the best part.

Return On Investment
• Greater Sales Efficiency
• Lower Cost per Opportunity
• Higher Conversion to Opportunity
• Shorter Sales Cycles
• Better Alignment Between Sales and Marketing

Six Ways to Know If You're Ready for Lead Scoring

If you're contemplating a lead-scoring system, but not sure if your organization is ready, here's a short checklist to help you determine if you're ready to move ahead.

1. **Do you have a lot of inquiries?**—Lead scoring is all about creating sales efficiency through the right priorities. If you don't have a lot of inquires coming in, you don't need to prioritize them because your sales team can get to all of them in the appropriate timeframe. In that case, your organization really won't benefit from lead scoring. But if you DO have a lot of inquiries coming in, and prioritization is a problem, a lead-scoring system can be invaluable to maximizing your revenue.

2. **Do you have a complex sale or an extended sales process?** Lead scoring only has a positive benefit if it creates more efficiency for your sales process. If your product is an impulse-buy, there is probably no reason to score leads. Prioritization becomes most effective and worthwhile when the leads are handed off to a lead-qualification team or the sales team. After all, if your rep spends 15-30 minutes per lead attempting contact, you don't want them chasing prospects who aren't ready to enter the sales cycle. Emails and outbound calls are better spent on the people who are most receptive to them.

3. **Do you have a CRM system?** Marketing automation without a CRM system is like a light bulb with no electricity: There's not much point! CRM is a tool for the sales rep to manage leads and clients. CRM systems

help the rep track engagement with a lead (such as making a call and sending outbound email). When you add in lead scoring, you've taken the power of CRM to a whole new level, because sales can logically prioritize who they call. Marketers sometimes ask, "Can't I do lead scoring and then just output a report from my marketing automation system and give it to the head of sales?" The answer is no: A queue of leads is not just a to-do list. Salespeople want to know "who's hot right now." When you have a lead-scoring system, the priority list is systematically changing throughout the day. If you're using a static spreadsheet for tracking, you miss the dynamic aspect that CRM provides. You simply won't get the ROI from your marketing automation system without pairing it with a good CRM.

4. **Do you have a marketing automation system?** "Can't we do lead scoring in CRM?" Not really. While it's technically possible to build some qualification formulas in CRM, they can't measure interest levels or digital body language—factors that are necessary for successful lead scoring. That's why the vast majority of lead scoring is done within the marketing automation system. That's where all the tools and technology for lead scoring are.

5. **Are your sales and marketing teams truly ready to establish cultural alignment?** Lead scoring helps marketing capture qualification information on the website and then pass that on to sales in a structured, prioritized way. If sales and marketing are trapped in the age-old argument ("All your leads suck" vs. "You don't follow up

on anything"), it's a positive indication that both groups could benefit from lead scoring. BUT: Are they willing to come together, have the important conversations, define the ideal customer profile, and share in the responsibilities of qualifying leads? Marketing must be willing to move beyond simply getting people to raise hands. They need to feel the passion of actually contributing to a sale. They must run campaigns that ultimately lead to revenue, not merely generate responses. On the other hand, if sales only wants as many leads as possible in any shape or form, and believes it's not marketing's job to do any qualification, they might not understand the value of lead scoring. A sales and marketing partnership for demand generation shares the roles and responsibilities for qualifying leads. Marketing is the matchmaker for sales. Sales starts the more intimate dating process and moves the relationship toward marriage.

6. **Do you have experienced resources?** Sales is good at moving prospects through a buying cycle and converting them into customers. Marketing is good at creating awareness and educating prospects on the benefits of buying products and services. But, most likely, no one on either team has ever tackled a systematic, analytical approach to qualification and scoring. Who will build, deploy, and train the team on the lead-scoring system (and maintain/update it)? The companies that are succeeding with lead scoring have experienced people to perform these vital duties. Yes, that's another plug for DemandGen. I couldn't resist.

MANUFACTURING DEMAND IN ACTION

Vistage International

Vistage International is the world's leading chief executive organization that provides essential coaching programs for CEOs and senior executives of small- to medium-sized businesses. Since the service is so appealing to both qualified and unqualified candidates, Vistage's marketing programs typically generate a large number of unqualified leads. This situation was wasting precious sales time as salespeople attempted to contact unqualified leads.

"We had constant tension between sales and marketing about the quality of the leads," said Carlo Saggese, vice president of application development. "At our Tuesday metrics meetings, we would report all these leads, and sales would say they were terrible, and I would be annoyed. We had no insight as to why these leads were terrible: They were just all terrible."

Detailed Process Develops Scoring Model for Qualification and Interest

Using a popular marketing automation system that enables lead scoring and nurturing, Vistage looked at what was available to rate the leads being sent to sales. To kick off that initiative, the company worked up an agreed-upon definition of a qualified lead, the right questions and answers to score leads, and how the information was presented within the CRM system. Vistage jumpstarted that process by asking its senior sales manager to essentially "sell a membership" to the team. Out of that role-playing, came the nuggets of information that were really important to ask. That led to a rating system for scoring the answers. "We laughed about how they did that. It was so natural," Saggese said.

With a qualification model established, the next step was to incorporate online behavior and enhance the scoring model to measure interest based on website visit frequency, depth of visits, email responsiveness, and activities such as downloading content, watching videos, and registering for events. "We modeled and ran scenarios of the questions and answers, which gave us a good feel for how scoring would work once implemented," said Saggese. "Now we had a scoring model that not only measures the qualification of a person, but the interest level as well." Service level agreements and processes were established and the Vistage sales team was trained to work only A and B leads, while C, D, and E leads remained with the marketing group to be flowed through nurturing campaigns until they are sales-ready.

Lead Conversion Jumps Significantly

Amid the worst economic times in recent history, Vistage's business grew significantly in 2009, largely due to the effectiveness of its lead scoring. Rather than waste time on unqualified leads, sales is now laser-focused on the right candidates. As a result, conversion grew from 44 percent to more than 60 percent in less than 10 months.

"Basically, if you are generating leads without lead scoring, I think you're wasting your time," Saggese says. "Your conversion rate goes up when sales focuses on the right leads—and when there's no animosity between the sales and marketing teams about what makes a lead qualified. What it boils down to is that we now have a common language that has changed our marketing behavior and brought us more qualified leads."

MANUFACTURING DEMAND IN ACTION

GAIN Capital

When you have a huge volume of leads and no method for lead prioritization, the only certainty is that you're leaving business on the table—a *lot* of business. Using a thoughtful lead-scoring model and strong nurturing program, $250 billion GAIN Capital Holdings achieved a whopping 20-percent reduction in sales conversion costs—with absolutely no overall decrease in conversion percentage. And in some regions, the company saw up to a 15-percent *increase* in conversion. Here's how they did it.

GAIN Capital—a global provider of online trading services specializing in foreign exchange—offers prospects a "practice account" that lets them learn to trade the foreign exchange market free for 30 days. It's a very effective approach that yields a very high volume of response. Historically, it was clear that practice account users and users from certain countries convert at higher rates than other leads—but that was only approximately 10 percent of total leads. The other 90 percent had no particular prioritization, and the volume made it impractical for sales to actually contact all these people. Yet sales received no compensation on any conversions unless they made contact. With the help of outside consultants, the team at GAIN developed a new lead-scoring model and integrated nurturing program.

Building the Solution: Data, Modeling, Testing

This approach was a complete change from GAIN's previous model. Knowing that sales' support would be critical to success, GAIN pulled together both its sales and marketing teams to build the new system, starting with data analysis. "We were blessed with a large volume of historical lead behavior and win/loss data that provided a strong basis upon which we could make fact-based decisions," said Emily Deadwyler, vice president of customer marketing and analytics. "Our analytical team used this data to build a predictive model for lead conversion."

The data analysis focused very heavily on practice account trading and website behavior, and uncovered a number of statistical trends that were tied with the sales team's hard-won insights to create the foundation for the new system. Working in partnership with key stakeholders and leveraging its wealth of data, GAIN created a lead-scoring worksheet to define the qualification criteria to be scored. After simulations and tests, the lead-scoring system ran in "silent mode" for about three months to confirm the approach and the "recipe" in the scoring model.

"We saw a few anomalies and made minor adjustments, but at this point we were able to provide hardcore numbers, substantiate the approach, win over the skeptics, and prove that lead scoring would be beneficial to the business,"

Deadwyler said. Today the lead-scoring model allows GAIN to measure the overall engagement level of a prospect, based on which effective nurturing decisions can be made automatically.

Reducing costs without impacting conversion

Over the course of a year, GAIN Capital has reduced its sales conversion costs by 20 percent—adding millions to the bottom line—while simultaneously expanding its offering into new regions and languages with *zero* decrease in overall conversion. Marketing operations have become much more effective. With automated and scoring-based nurturing email programs, the marketing team can provide personalized messaging to prospects that previously simply would not qualify for a sales contact. That's improved customer experiences while generating demand. And the positive results of the sales and marketing alignment are being felt across both organizations.

KEY TAKEAWAYS

- Lead scoring is usually a combination of *fitness* and *interest*.

- There are four types of lead scoring:
  - Interest-Only
  - Qualification-Only
  - Two-Dimensional
  - Predictive

- There are two types of information that affect lead scoring:
  - Explicit—The attributes provided by the prospect
  - Implicit—The information we can infer based on activity

- Building a qualification model:
  - Ask sales and marketing to describe the perfect customer.
  - Update your forms to capture information that confirms/disconfirms qualification.

- Lead scoring at a glance:
  - Identify two to four qualitative criteria to measure qualification.
  - Identify the online behaviors that correlate with prospect interest.
  - Use both measurements to set a rating for each new inquiry.
  - Ensure that the right scoring hand-off processes exists between sales and marketing.
  - Create a simple and effective way to show the scored leads in your CRM.
  - Gather at least one quarter's worth of scoring data and analyze scoring distribution through to closed/won opportunities.
  - Implement a qualitative feedback loop with sales to refine the model.

- Present scored leads in the CRM system using a highly visual, at-a-glance interface that requires no training.

- Ensure there's explicit agreement in the form of SLAs between sales and marketing about what each party will do with a lead at each stage.

- Keep things fresh by constantly reexamining your qualification questions and weightings.

© 2012 DemandGen International, Inc.

Chapter 6

LEAD NURTURING: THE PAYOFF FOR PATIENT MARKETERS

I hope I'm not shocking you with this revelation about the sales and marketing process, but, despite even your team's very best efforts, most of your leads aren't necessarily going to proceed in an orderly fashion from inquiry through to qualification on to being accepted and then into the closed/won status. No duh, right? It's just a fact we all live with. However, if you apply the principles I'm sharing, the net impact can be a dramatic increase in the percentage of conversions. That means more customers and more revenue.

There's one more key practice to share to improve conversions, and it's equally—if not more—important than lead scoring. It's *lead nurturing*.

So what creates the momentum for a lead to move along its journey through the Demand Funnel? At a high level, the prospect's willingness to proceed through the buying process will either come from his own initiative to move through each stage, or it will come from you proactively maintaining a conversation with him. No doubt, the sales team will guide prospects through the latter stages of the funnel, but at the top, where the funnel is widest and where sales is typically not yet engaged, lead nurturing is a vital part of creating and maintaining that momentum.

So, what, exactly, *is* lead nurturing? Here's an expanded definition: It's the automated process of engaging in a two-way dialogue with prospects to provide and obtain the information each party needs at key stages of the buying cycle. The ultimate goal of lead nurturing is to help prospects understand that your product or service is the best choice to achieve their objectives. Let's look more deeply at the key points of this definition.

- **Engage in a dialogue with prospects**—Just sending a lot of emails to prospects to stay top-of-mind does not constitute true *engagement*. When we talk about engagement, we mean *two-way* communication that respects the prospect's time, interests, and preferences. Engagement means not only what you communicate *to them*, but also listening carefully to *what they communicate to you* through their digital body language. Be sure to take into account the feedback you receive from prospects, both explicit and implicit, and adapt your communications accordingly.

Engagement means *dialogue*, not *monologue*. It means creating communication that has value for *both* parties, so that buyer and seller both have an interest in continuing to communicate.

- **Gauge each stage of the buying process**—Unless your product is an impulse purchase, your prospect goes through a multistage process before making a purchase decision. Remember, the prospect's *buying* process is not the same as your *selling* process! Typically, the buying process looks like this:

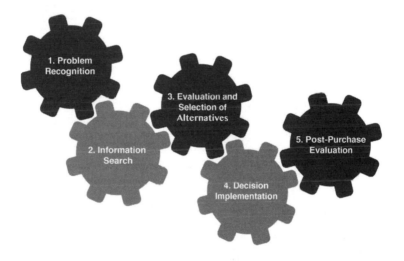

Figure 6.1 The Five Key Stages of the B2B Buying Process

A good starting point for your lead nurturing programs is to clearly identify the points within the buying process where prospects can be helped by receiving useful information from you. Step 2 in the above diagram might seem obvious, but, in reality, your prospects can probably benefit from *relevant* information before and after **every** stage of the buying process—including the first and last stages.

The key word is ***relevant.*** For your particular product or service, it's important to define exactly what kind of information is relevant at each stage (we'll discuss that issue later).

Of course, it can get complicated quickly, because most companies have more than one product and more than one kind of customer. And, for most companies, these stages aren't clean little boxes: They are multistep mini-processes in themselves. So it's important to take appropriate time to sketch out the buying processes for the specific buyer personas and identify specific product/service resources that align with those needs.

- **Help prospects achieve their objectives**—Why do prospects become customers? Ultimately, it's because they feel and decide your solution will help them achieve their objectives. They believe that yours is the best choice, for various reason(s), to solve their problem.

In terms of content strategy for nurtures, the key point is that lead nurturing needs to be about *the buyer*—**not** about *you*. Too often, we see lead-nurture programs that are completely focused on product features—the "what" and "how"—and not on the benefits—the "why"—which are far more important. Of course features are important, but nurturing is as much about igniting feelings as about sharing facts. It's rooted in biology that decisions, particularly "yes" buying decisions, are largely based on emotions. A one-to-one dialogue that starts with "why" ensures the prospect will connect with you faster. Starting with "how" forces the prospect to tally up a bunch of features to figure out what to do and determine if you're the best choice. By starting with "why," you create an emotional connection with the prospect first and that connection will later foster greater interest in learning about the "what" and "how."

Here's what I mean. Which of the following two approaches is a more powerful introduction to a conversation?

We believe that managing your diabetes should be painless and easier. We want to help you to live a long, healthy life without the hassles of testing your blood sugars manually. So, we created Dialife for you. It's an automated way to monitor your blood sugars 24 hours a day without ever pricking your finger. Want to see how?

– OR –

Get Dialife. It's a continuous glucose monitor that you place on your arm that uses laser beams to check your blood sugar level instead of traditional blood testing. It's about the size of your thumb and is covered by most insurance companies. Watch this demo to learn more.

The Five Goals of Lead Nurturing

- Accelerate the sales process by moving prospects through a structured buying cycle.
- Keep your company/solution top-of-mind.
- Reveal your benefits in serialized sound-bites.
- Capture qualification profiles.
- Measure and increase the prospect's interest.

IT'S A PROCESS

In fleshing out our definition some more, perhaps we've glossed over an important point. The first portion of the lead-nurturing definition is perhaps the most important: "*automated process.*" Lead nurturing is an ongoing, continual process that's driven by systems, schedules, and programmed guidelines. It's not a one-shot deal. The structure of every nurture framework is unique. Good nurtures are the opposite of batch-and-blast marketing. They are carefully constructed with a variety of facets to gently but firmly drive prospects to very clearly defined goals. In many organizations, the proper practice is to establish *multiple* types of nurture programs that pursue different objectives:

- **Seed Nurturing**—These nurtures are aimed at contacts "above the funnel" (sometimes called "suspects"). Here, we are targeting new contacts by acquiring names, lists, and opt-in email addresses and creating multi-touch campaigns to encourage/persuade these new people to engage with us. This multi-touch concept is distinctly different than the old-school "one-and-done" approach, where we simply built the *campaign du jour* and tried to get responses through "another random act of marketing." Experience tells us that a single exposure is usually insufficient to build the level of awareness required to generate a response. Instead, our strategy is to build a *series of touches* that work in concert to build brand recognition, deliver content the suspect cares about, and increase awareness among the total available market. The old adage "There's no silver bullet" is still relevant today. Instead, we want to build a series of one or two touches a month targeted to our suspects (a so-called "drip-nurture"). A bad response or no response typically only means "not now." However, be careful not to overdo it with too-frequent emails. Over-communicating can make you come across like a stalker. Nobody wants to feel forced into a relationship. Your goal is to provide valuable content and resources, not make them cringe at the sight of another email from you. Think, "Can I offer you a drink?" instead of "Can I take you home?"

- **Inquiry Nurturing**—An inquiry nurture continues the conversation with someone who has responded to a seed nurture. The prospect enters the funnel as an *Inquiry* and begins to receive communications focused on educating this new prospect to increase their interest. Done right, this top-of-funnel nurture further qualifies the prospect before an introduction is made to a lead development rep or sales rep.

- **Marketing Qualified Lead (MQL) Nurturing**—In the MQL lead nurture, the goal now is to see if the qualified lead will engage with a rep. Since an MQL is showing substantial interest based on the scoring system, the prospect is likely at a later stage in the buying process and might be ready to discuss their needs and your solution in more depth. This nurture can have a huge impact on movement down that funnel because it "automagically" tries to engage with the MQL instead of waiting for sales to reach out when they get around to it. Although it's automated, an effective technique is to have the drip emails appear to come directly from the assigned rep to the MQL. This assignment is typically made using the CRM's lead assignment rules, and since the two systems are integrated, we can have the emails dynamically come from the assigned sales or lead development rep. The calls to action for these one-to-one emails might be to set up an introductory phone call, schedule a short demo, provide a free consultation, or offer a free trial (among other common tactics). Assuming you have lead scoring in place, the MQL nurtures are only initiated with qualified leads that have demonstrated they fit the qualification criteria and have shown a medium-to-high level of interest. (see Chap. 5).

Certainly, you could build nurtures for other stages of the funnel, but the inquiry and MQL stages are great places to start. Before we move on, I want to suggest that, after you get the default inquiry and MQL nurtures in place, consider building custom nurture tracks *within* each one that target your individual personas. For example, if your MQL nurture commonly has two or three different personas (based on industry, role, or company size), you might develop a separate track for each of them that contains content designed to help that persona move further through the funnel.

Customized persona-based nurture tracks for prospects at each funnel stage enable you to better address your prospect's concerns and requirements, instead of just falling back on the default track and standard message. An automated message coming from the rep that reads, "If you're concerned about the security of your patient data..." will be more effective to a health-care prospect than a generic one like, "Data security is a key issue in companies similar to yours...." Start with a basic nurture and then build custom tracks within it once the nurture is up and running and your personas are well-defined in the system. Now, let's look at how you can nurture when contacts fall outside the funnel.

- **Recycle Nurturing**—Suppose that, after sales receives the MQL, the rep attempts to reach the prospect several times by email and possibly phone over a few weeks. What happens then? Although 90 percent of leads don't convert into closed/won business, that doesn't mean they have no future value. They still need to "go somewhere" in our funnel. So, if he fails to make contact, the rep should designate the lead for *recycling* in the CRM, selecting one of several predefined reasons (e.g. bad timing, lack of budget, competitive losses.) A recycling nurture lets the prospect "snooze" for some period of time, and then gives marketing the opportunity to try again for a response by providing information targeted to the recycling reason. For example "bad timing" might indicate the need for a longer/slower nurture or content about why the time is right for your solution. For "lack of budget" you could offer an ROI calculator and customer case studies on how your solution has been cost-effective. (You can see a video on how this works on the manufacturingdemand.com website.)

- **Tactical Nurturing**—Sometimes, we nurture for a specific, tactical reason.For example, if you offer a free trial, such a campaign might benefit from a well-defined, thoughtful nurture program to encourage the prospect to download and install the product and give feedback. You can nudge them along during their trial period with screenshots or video walkthroughs showing what they can do with the product and how they will benefit from it. Toward the end of the trial period, your emails can include a "countdown clock" to create a sense of urgency. Other examples of tactical nurtures include automated subscription renewals or event nurturing to handle the series of invitations and reminders.

- **Onboarding Nurturing**—You did it. You have a new customer. This is a great time to build upon the relationship with a post-purchase nurture, welcoming your new customer and show the valuable resources available. Many B-to-C marketers really shine here, while I've found that B-to-B companies often overlook this key opportunity to build rapport with new customers around training, support, and feedback.

- **Customer Lifecycle Nurturing**—If your company sells more than one product or service, it's essential to maintain the conversation throughout the customer lifecycle. This also lets you execute vital upsell/cross-sell campaigns.

THE BASIC RECIPE FOR A LEAD NURTURE

The best analogy for a well-designed lead nurture is that it's a *conversation* between you and your prospect. And remember: A conversation is a two-way street. So, what's the best way to initiate, structure, and sustain a lead nurturing program? After working on hundreds of these programs, I find there's a basic "recipe" that almost any enterprise can implement to succeed and it involves the following elements:

- **A defined objective**—What do you want the prospect to do or to know by the time your nurture ends? Establish very specific, measurable objectives for every nurture. Otherwise, how can you determine how well it did? If you can't define a specific, measurable objective, you won't be able to determine if the nurture is working. An example of a vague objective is "Increase awareness of our company/product." A better objective is "Convert 5 percent of free trial users into paid subscribers." Another measurable objective might be to move 8 percent of inquiries to MQL status. Segmentation techniques help you determine how many of the people who entered the nurture achieved the desired goal and, therefore, how effective the nurture was.

- **Entry Criteria**—Here, we have a lot of specific questions that we should address to aid in the design phase. How will contacts feed into the program—by contact group, filter, status, or form submission? Can a contact enter the program more than once? Are there differences between the initial feed of contacts and any subsequent or ongoing feeds? What are the specific field requirements for identifying personas? What contacts should be excluded from the program, and how should they be handled? Are there different exit paths for different exclusions?

- **Exit Criteria**—We don't want a "Hotel California" nurture program ("You can check out any time you like, but you can never leave"). So we need to decide under what conditions contacts should be removed from the program. Is it when they complete the program or when they achieve the goal? What other use cases should cause an exit? For example, how will you handle unsubscribe requests, hard-bounces, successful registrations, or changes to record type in the CRM system? The trick is to build a list of the conditions that would remove people from the nurture.

- **Touchpoints/Key Messages**—Do you envision only one track for contacts entering the program, or will you need different tracks for unique personas? If there are multiple tracks, how will the content and timings differ? How many touchpoints will there be for each track? What is the key message and call to action for each touchpoint? For nurtures that use more than email, what additional types of touches will occur—such as SMS text message, call-on-demand, direct mail piece, or even social media posts.

- **Frequency/Timing**—Is there a waiting period at the beginning of the program before any evaluations are performed or emails are sent? What about at the end of the program? What is the waiting period between touchpoints/emails? Are there day/time restrictions to account for business hours and locations? Are there conditions where someone should skip a touchpoint?

- **Assets Required**—This is a crucial component of any type of nurture program: the content. Are landing pages or fulfillment material (such as white papers or case studies) needed? Do those materials already exist? How many emails must be created, and what type of template will you use? If these assets don't exist, who is responsible for creating them? If these assets will be gated by forms, don't forget to define the requirements for the forms, such as campaign ID, fields used, pre-population, or progressive profiling. If the assets will be housed on new landing pages, be sure to establish responsibility for creating those pages.

- **Reporting Requirements**—How will you measure the success of the nurture? If a an objective was well-defined, be sure you know upfront how you will measure it. You want specific, defined metrics in order to track results and identify the reports you want to see and how often.

- **Post-Nurture Plan**—Think about what happens to prospects after they exit the nurture. Have a plan for them, such as flowing them into another nurture. Remember, you may have more than one post-nurture outcome, depending on whether they exit in the middle or at the conclusion of the program.

NURTURING THROUGH THE FUNNEL

Remember that, when considering a product or service, buyers go through a multistage buying process that can be a fast cycle or a lengthy and complex process, depending on the product. During this process, the buyer looks for and needs different kinds of information to help with the decision.

A Nurture Project Brief

Before you initiate a nurture program, it can be very helpful to perform some preliminary analysis and strategy definition. I like to create a "Nurture Project Brief" that responds to the issues above and contains some or all of the following elements:

1. **Overview**—Articulate a summary of the initiative in general terms, including relevant contextual background information that is important to understanding the entire nurture project.

2. **Project Summary**—Summarize the project's steps and include a timeline.

3. **Nurture Objectives**—Define a specific set of measurable goals. What are the key performance metrics that will demonstrate the success of the nurture program?

4. **Tone and Personality**—What will be the voice, tone, and manner of the nurture communications and fulfillment/response materials?

5. **Marketing Assets Required**—What content will you need? List the assets required such as white papers, data sheets, demos, and more.

6. **Approvals**—Whose buy-in will you need to initiate and sustain the program?

7. **Define the Specifics**—Will this be single- or multi-track? How many touches will there be? What's the duration? What are the entry and exit criteria? Are there special exit paths or late-entry on-ramps? Next, dive down to the details of each touch: the template, content summary, landing page requirements, assets required, timing, and more.

At first, the buyer is typically interested in general information: How do I solve my problem? Then, he looks at different products or services to learn how they approach that problem.

Next, the focus narrows to products or services that seem best suited to the challenge. The buyer examines them more deeply, looking at details of implementation or usage, reviews, risks, price, and more.

Next, he makes the selection. He decides on one solution and goes through the purchase process.

Finally, he implements that solution, ensures it works properly, keeps it updated, and addresses any subsequent issues.

As you use nurturing to move a prospect through the demand funnel from inquiry to closed sale and beyond, you should have one goal in mind: to provide the specific, relevant information that your prospect needs at each stage. This is where you have to begin translating the buying stages into the stages of your demand funnel, so you can identify the right information to deliver at the right time.

Figure 6.2 shows five points where nurturing is particularly effective in delivering the right information to prospects and driving them through the funnel or back into it.

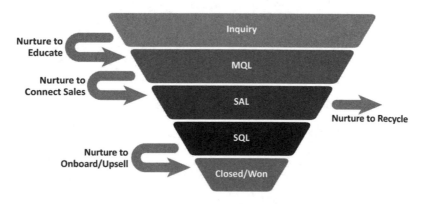

Figure 6.2: Key Places for Nurturing Programs

PHASE ONE: INQUIRY TO MQL: IT'S ALL ABOUT EDUCATION

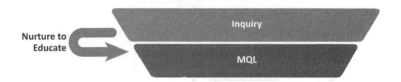

Moving the prospect through the inquiry stage to become a Marketing Qualified Lead (MQL) is actually a process of education. Make sure your nurtures are focused on educating the prospect about your solution, but with an emphasis on the prospect's needs. This is sometimes described as "welcome nurturing," but it should definitely be much more than that. This stage is your greatest opportunity to engage with your prospect and generate real, sustained interest in your offering. Educational/welcome nurtures are the right place to use your exciting multimedia content, webinars, and other similar resources as calls to action.

Depending on the nature of your business, you may need multiple nurtures to address the specific needs of different kinds of prospects. Within each of those nurtures, there may be numerous tracks or paths that your prospect may take, depending on his digital body language. For example, a software company likely has several different software products, and each of those may be used by different kinds of businesses with different types of challenges. The more specifically you address your prospect's needs, the better success you will have at moving the prospect on through the funnel.

PHASE TWO: MQL TO SAL: MAKE THE CONNECTION

The next step in the nurturing process is to move the lead from MQL to Sales Accepted (sales-ready) Lead (SAL) status. The primary goal is to connect the prospect with a lead development rep or salesperson. The best content assets and lures at this stage are tools like needs assessments, free consultations, and personal demonstrations—anything that results in communication between the prospect and a representative who can answer questions and help with engagement to take the relationship to the next level. People buy from people and companies they like, so engaging with contacts in one-on-one conversations moves the buying process along in most cases.

PHASE THREE: SAL AND SQL: RECYCLE

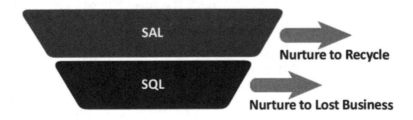

There's nothing left for marketing to do once the lead achieves SAL or Sales Qualified Lead (SQL) stages, right? Think again! We need a plan for leads that are accepted by sales, but turn out to be not yet ready. In many organizations, these leads simply fall through the cracks, and that's an unbelievable waste. After all, if they weren't MQLs, they wouldn't have gotten this far, so they still have long-term value. Send these leads into your recycle nurture program that gets them back through the Demand Funnel and reengaged with sales in the future. If you don't, a huge percentage of these contacts will buy from a competitor because you didn't stay engaged with them. They may not be ready to speak to a rep at the MQL stage, but, by recycling, marketing can stay engaged with the prospect while sales focuses on MQLs that *are* engaging.

What about lost business? Sales Qualified Leads are lost for a variety of reasons, and most of them don't mean that the lead won't have future value one way or another. Your company may have other solutions that could benefit the prospect. The prospect's chosen solution (from your competitor) might not work out. It's honestly very rare that an SQL should be disqualified in the database. A better approach is to put them into a win-back nurture that puts them in hibernation for a period and checks in to ask, "How are things going?"

PHASE FOUR: SQL TO CLOSED/WON: ONBOARDING, RETENTION, AND UPSELL

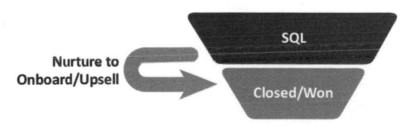

Woo-hoo, you've won the business! But don't relax: Your job's not done. As we all know, it's a lot more expensive to get a new customer than to keep an old one, so now it's up to you to keep building rapport and onboarding nurtures are a great way to achieve that.

Start with a "welcome aboard" nurture for net-new customers, followed by onboarding and training nurtures. If your solution is complex, or customers can use guidance on adoption, direct them to customer resources like your online community, resource center, or training videos. At the right time, upsell and cross-sell campaigns are clearly good choices for future nurture campaigns as well.

Continuing nurtures for loyalty and retention often include gentle reminders about ongoing training, invitations to events and webinars, user group communications, and industry news/trends. The goal is to keep your company top-of-mind throughout the customer lifecycle and help ensure customers get what they were promised in the buying cycle. We all enjoy the upscale hotels where the maid turns down the bed and delivers your nightly chocolate, the concierge calls after you check in to see if everything is OK, and the bellman demos all the hotel room options. Why not do your own "virtual version" of hotel-style customer service with your onboarding nurtures?

WHY LEAD NURTURING MATTERS: SIX REASONS

If you're like most marketers who understand the value and power of marketing automation, chances are you need no convincing that lead nurturing is a good idea. But you *are* likely to have colleagues and management who aren't as aware of the impact lead nurturing can have on the buying cycle and, ultimately, revenue. For those folks in your enterprise who need some convincing metrics to become believers, here are some helpful stats from a few of the most trusted benchmarking firms:

1. Companies that excel at lead nurturing generate 50 percent more sales-ready leads at 33 percent lower cost per lead (Forrester Research).

2. Nurtured leads produce a 20-percent increase in sales opportunities over non-nurtured leads (Demand Gen Report).

3. Sixty percent of marketers believe that technology can help them develop more high-quality leads (Forrester Research).

4. Sales reps dedicate 14 percent of their time to lead development, but only 6.3 percent of leads are utilized (Sirius Decisions).

5. Nearly 80 percent of marketing leads never convert into sales. Lack of lead nurturing is the common cause of this poor performance (MarketingSherpa).

6. Eighty-four percent of qualified leads are not ready to buy (Aberdeen Research).

The Key Tactics of Lead Nurturing

- Internalize the Demand Funnel.
- Decide which types of nurtures to build to support the funnel.
- Develop a nurture brief that includes clear objectives.
- Inventory your existing content.
- Map existing and future content to buying-cycle stages.
- Design the workflow processes using a diagramming or flowchart tool before you begin program development.
- Measure effectiveness of the nurtures and optimize for the desired results.

© 2012 DemandGen International, Inc.

CONTENT: HAVING THE RIGHT BAIT

One of the principal tenets of Manufacturing Demand is that you need to speak in different ways to different buyers at different phases of the sales cycle. In fishing vernacular, you need lots of different lures and lots of different kinds of bait to catch lots of different fish. Your buyer personas will help you understand these delineations very well. Remember Gary (the broker) and Maria (the loan officer) from my ride-alongs with Joe at Ellie Mae? They have different pain points, different needs, and different motivations—so catching them is going to require different bait.

For instance, early in the buying cycle, a technology evaluator might want to sign up for an e-newsletter or download a white paper that helps educate him regarding the key characteristics of an emerging technology. Later in the cycle, he might register for a webinar or download a product demo. If a VP-titled site visitor downloads your ROI calculator, it's a signal that the company has moved further through the buying cycle. You want to ensure you have the right content for the right stakeholders at the right time to *help* them through the buying cycle.

Once you've structured your Demand Funnel and lead nurture programs, just what, exactly, are *you* going to say to your prospects as they wind their way through your Demand Funnel? A good way to start is to think about what types of content you have—and where each type fits in your funnel.

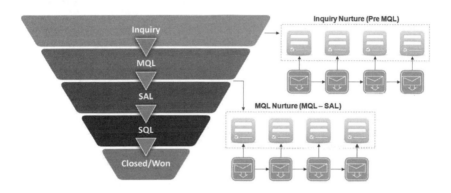

Traditional content-marketing strategy across industries used to involve marketers creating broad ranges of content, such as data sheets, white papers, and much more. That content was typically designed to tell prospects about the products and services you offer: what they do, why they are better than others, how to use them.

Yawn.

Today's sophisticated B2B buyers don't want that kind of content anymore (or at least not primarily). They're looking for helpful *educational* content that makes them more knowledgeable—and incidentally also makes them feel like your company is a respected thought leader in its sector. Robust, compelling content—that is more about the buyer and less about the seller—is what fills the funnel.

Demand generation today is a constant process of developing content to attract your target buyer. If you don't continually refresh your "bait locker," changing out your offerings and expanding your selection, the fish will lose interest and (to carry this metaphor to an extreme) things are not going to smell very good. Remember, there are a lot of other fisherman trolling the lake, so your bait needs to be the most appealing.

Content marketing strategy is a serious discipline involving the planning, creation, delivery, and management of informational content. A content strategy defines messaging, purpose, structure, workflow, and governance for content across the organization. A content strategist is analogous to a creative director: the former for content, the latter for design. Two points of content strategy are particularly relevant to marketing automation: frequency and relevance.

- **Frequency**—Content generation and dissemination must maintain momentum to be effective.

  - **Frequency of contact**—Strive for the balance point by delivering updates that are frequent enough to maintain interest, without becoming incessant and annoying.

  - **Frequency of content updates**—Keep things fresh by producing new materials often—and not forgetting to cull the pieces that are outdated and stale.

- **Relevance**—Marketing automation systems, data segmentation, and personas enable you to pinpoint your messaging to specific targets. Take advantage of that ability.

- **Relevance to buyer interest**—Messages should focus on the buyer's challenges, needs, concerns, and issues, as opposed to the solution being offered or broad generic topics.

- **Relevance to buying stage**—Materials and messages are designed to fit the buyer's current stage in the buying cycle.

- **Relevance to marketing requirements**—It can't be relevant if it's not there. Audit all your existing material and document it in a content inventory workbook or system. You'll find out where the balance is off and what gaps exist that need to be filled.

Top Tips for Content Curation

1. Perform a content audit and document the content inventory.

2. Develop key themes, taking into account buyer personas and product positioning.

3. Assess content resources, defining the who/what/where/when of content development.

4. Create content, calling on appropriate resources for research, development, review, and approval.

5. Publish content through appropriate means.

6. Track, maintain, and revise content regularly.

MANUFACTURING DEMAND IN ACTION

Ellie Mae, Inc.'s On-Board Nurture Program

Since 2003, Ellie Mae has redefined the market for software and services in the often-fragmented residential mortgage industry by bringing together mortgage bankers, credit unions, community banks, mortgage brokers, lenders, and service providers. Its acclaimed Encompass software delivers a comprehensive solution to support brokers and bankers throughout the loan process.

But Ellie Mae considers the sale of the software license to be the starting line—not the finish line. Crucial post-sale adoption processes—the "on-boarding" of the customer—must take place to ensure a successful long-term partnership with the customer. For many users, Encompass is more feature-rich than what they're used to. Although it's easy and intuitive to use, it can be intimidating at first. With tens of thousands of customer contacts and a small marketing team, the challenge was significant.

The solution? A comprehensive, highly structured on-boarding nurture program that helps users through their first their initial months with Encompass. This automated welcome program lets the company reach users right at the point when they've starting using the software and continue to stay in touch throughout their initial use of the software.

Ellie Mae created two on-board nurtures—one for system administrators that focuses on key configuration steps, and one for users that focuses on the resources and training new users might want to use Encompass to its fullest potential.

Through integration with its marketing automation system, Ellie Mae automatically adds users to the program in less than 24 hours after their first login. Already, the company has synched and segmented contact data for more than 30,000 users at the right time—just using a few mouse clicks and without burdening the company's IT staff. From there, it's a series of timed, orchestrated emails at different rates, depending on their role (admin or user). For instance, users see the following steps:

- **Start**—An overview of new-user recommendations.
- **Learn**—A review of different training options.
- **Ask**—How to get on-demand and one-to-one customer support.
- **Explore**—How different users can be more efficient in Encompass.
- **Health Check**—A check-in to see if users are on track.
- **Tell Us**—An opportunity to give feedback.

These emails drive recipients to the company's dedicated Client Resource Center where they can get more training, tips, tools, support, and more. By getting users engaged with Encompass and adopting more of its features, Ellie Mae is improving customer satisfaction and long-term loyalty. Users are more aware of on-demand service options as well as the availability of add-on purchase options. There are also fewer costly calls to the support center. The on-boarding has also led to a 60-percent increase in the rate that users return to key service pages. The bounce rate for those pages has also plummeted, indicating that users are spending quality time with these online resources.

STAGE	AWARENESS	EDUCATION	EVALUATION	JUSTIFICATION	PURCHASE	POST-PURCHASE
What prospect is doing	Beginning solution search	Has identified key solutions and is examining each	Evaluating solutions against needs	Assembling short list	Has made selection and is ready to buy	Using, updating, upgrading/expanding
What prospect is asking	• Who are the suppliers for my need? • What's the scope of potential? • Where do I stand? • How can I easily find out more?	• What do they offer? • Are their customers achieving success? • Do they fit my need? • How can I easily evaluate/demo?	• Do they meet my expectations? • What do analysts say? • Is the company viable? • How do they compare? • Why should I choose? • What's the cost?	• Is this a leading, solid product/company? • Does it meet or exceed my need? • Can I afford to buy and implement?	• How can I easily purchase? • Who can I call? • Why buy now? • Do they have a partner in my area?	• How do I get training for my people? • What resources and information are available? • How/why should I upgrade? • What other options/related solutions are there?
Best content types	• Industry white papers • Company product white papers • Customer stories • Assessment tests • Press releases	• Company white paper • Seminar/ presentation • Product spec sheets • Customer stories • Recorded demo • Analyst reports • Educational tips	• Features/benefits • Free trials • Webinar/ live demo • Competitive and cost comparisons • Company/product recognition/ awards	• Product/customer reference site • ROI tools • Product awards • Customer stories • Press releases • Webinar/ presentation • Live demo or sales call	• Direct sales • Partner locator • Promotions or deals • Service and support information	• Training and user information • Service and support information • Cross-sell/upsell • User community • Industry/thought leadership

KEY TAKEAWAYS

- Not every lead proceeds through the Demand Funnel at the planned pace. Lead nurturing guides these leads through the funnel by offering the right information to the right person at the right time.

- Nurture campaigns should be about the *buyer*, not the *seller*.

- The Five Goals of Lead Nurturing
  - Accelerate the sales process by moving prospects through a structured buying cycle.
  - Keep your company/solution top-of-mind.
  - Reveal your benefits in serialized sound-bites.
  - Capture qualification profiles.
  - Measure and increase the prospect's interest.

- Nurture campaigns include seed, inquiry, and MQL—each of which requires different content, timings, and tone.

- So-called "tactical" nurtures help with specific goals such as on-boarding.

- Recycle nurtures move leads back up the Demand Funnel for further nurturing because they are not ready to buy.

- Make sure you have defined objectives, entry criteria, and exit criteria for your nurtures. Define the key messages, timings, and content assets required—and have a post-nurture plan as well.

- Have the right "Content Bait"
  - Frequency
  - Relevance

The CMO explains marketing's contribution

Chapter 7

ANALYTICS: KEEPING SCORE OF YOUR SUCCESS

Do you know why sales gets the big bucks? Because revenue can be directly attributed to their performance. Can marketing's performance be tied to revenue? Finally, the answer is *yes*! Every marketer who boards "the transformation train"—even the creative team—needs to know that the ability to measure and report on marketing's impact on revenue is essential to change the perception of marketing from a cost center into a revenue generator. More than half of all CMOs say their top challenge is quantifying and measuring the value of the marketing programs they execute and the investments they make (CMO Council: Marketing Outlook 2008).

A marketing automation system that's integrated with CRM enables us to measure performance "from click to close." Here's the thing: When you start to apply scientific precision to your processes for capturing, scoring, nurturing, and closing prospects, you're going to capture a heck of a lot of data. Conveniently, the data we capture on prospects as part of the process of "Manufacturing Demand" also contains the quantifications and measurements that we can use to demonstrate the value of our activities. Although the fact that you're amassing a ton of data is daunting, it's a good thing for marketers—because it also contains the metrics that matter.

The path to demonstrating marketing's contribution to revenue starts with rigorously analyzing marketing performance and measuring how effective your marketing campaigns have been and how much they've contributed to the pipeline and to revenue. To get the respect we deserve as marketers, we must show how we *actively drive revenue and profits*. It's essential to define and deliver the **right** metrics that demonstrate the value of your marketing team—as well as to help you better target and refine your efforts.

Evolving into a metrics-driven marketing culture takes a commitment to assigning resources for defining those metrics and reporting them. A marketing operations team—your "marketing geeks"—provides the central focus that's needed. This team is an internal, dedicated resource for developing and orchestrating the processes and systems that enable efficient and effective marketing. More specifically, marketing operations staff members must develop and manage the internal marketing processes that ensure smooth strategic planning, financial management, marketing performance measurement (including dashboard development), marketing infrastructure, and overall marketing excellence.

BUT WHAT SHOULD YOU MEASURE?
START WITH THE END

I could fill a bookshelf or two with books devoted solely to the topic of marketing metrics. However, none of the ones I've read give the specifics or examples to guide you on Demand Funnel metrics, campaign attribution, lead-scoring dashboards, or how to set up effective reporting for showing marketing's ultimate contribution to revenue. I'll gladly help you get started on *what* to measure and report on, but, sadly, there's no simple solution to showing you *how* to measure. The *how* isn't hard. It's just that every marketing system is different, and I'd have to dedicate separate chapters to cover each of the leading systems. Instead, I'll offer some specific advice on what you need to do to capture those measurements.

So where do you start? You start with the end in mind. That's worth repeating: *You start with the end in mind.* Build a set of PowerPoint slides or Excel reports that show what you want to measure and report on. Then, reverse engineer your systems and data-capture requirements and processes so you collect the data you'll need to report on. For example, if you want a pie chart showing each key channel's contribution to MQL volume, then you need to capture the channel that MQL originated from. That means you need to capture the originating channel on form submission, pass that data over to the CRM on lead creation, and preserve it when the lead is converted to an SQL. Making that process happen is not necessarily hard using today's systems, but the point is that you must start with what you want to report on, and *then* figure how and where to capture it for reporting.

Since the focus of this book is on manufacturing demand and lead management, I'll stick to what you need to measure in these areas, but I'll also provide some other resources that will help you in other areas. Be sure to check out the book's website, *www.manufacturingdemand.com,* for additional resources and updates, including a few spreadsheet templates and screen shots to get you started. Depending on the complexity of your environment and what marketing automation system and CRM system you use, you may also need a separate business intelligence (BI) tool to aggregate and analyze your data. Many will find they can get by with the reporting/analysis tools integrated within the marketing automation and/or CRM systems they've chosen to implement.

THERE IS NO GAAP FOR MARKETING

Let's start with the bad news: Marketing analysis is still characterized by some very rough terrain. Unlike financial analytics, there are few (if any) agreed-upon standards and definitions for measuring and assessing marketing performance. There are no "generally accepted accounting principles" (GAAP) or standard reports for marketing (as there are for finance), so models, comparisons, and benchmarks across different organizations are scarce and have inherent limitations.

What's more, there are no commercial ready-made solutions. Instead, we're seeing a broad assortment of *tools* that our marketing geeks can apply. And, we should sadly acknowledge the parallel truth with respect to presentation tools for marketing analytics: Microsoft Excel and PowerPoint are here to stay. Their utility and ubiquity mean that we marketers must accept their limitations in exchange for low-cost adoptability.

THE THREE C'S VS. "THE BOOTH LOOKED GREAT"

But there's good news, too. The mountains of data we're accumulating in our marketing automation and CRM systems—the clicks, the downloads, the pageviews, the forwards—it collectively holds the insights we need to demonstrate the value of marketing in concrete, measurable ways.

Measure what you can base decisions on. And measure what you will be asked to prove: namely, marketing's contribution to pipeline and revenue. If you're asked how the tradeshow went, the right answer is *not*, "The booth looked great." The *right* answer should be, "The booth looked great, it was well attended by our target market, our efforts generated 127 inquires that are going through a post-show nurture, and 12 MQLs have been handed off to sales."

To be effective in tracking and reporting, we need to focus our efforts on what I call "The Three C's" of marketing analytics:

- What can you *Count?*
- What *Counts?*
- What can you *Count* on?

Unlike the days of estimating billboard impressions and readership reports, you can count virtually everything going on in marketing today. So *what you can count* is easy. *What counts* is more subjective, but, at a minimum, you'll want to track channels, lead sources, campaigns, asset consumption, funnel metrics, lead score distribution, and contribution to pipeline and revenue. *What you can count on* depends on three things: how well you set up your tracking systems, how consistent your marketing efforts are in showing predictable trends, and how well-integrated your MA and CRM system are to pass the right data through "from click to close."

THE THREE CATEGORIES OF MARKETING ANALYTICS

More good news: You probably don't need to track and calculate as many analytic measures as you think. Your car has thousands of parts, but just a few dashboard displays. The weatherman gives a forecast in five minutes despite an enormous amount meteorological data available. Similarly, when our counterpart—the CFO—presents information to the board of directors, only a few key financial indicators are discussed: the P&L statement, the status of accounts receivable, EBITDA, cash balances, inventory, and maybe a few other business-specific or industry-related yardsticks. Clearly, the accounting pros have vast amounts of information in their accounting systems, but through experience over time, financial experts have determined these are the most important and relevant reports and metrics.

As marketers, we need the same approach in defining our own key performance indicators. These include marketing's total impact on pipeline (the funnel), revenue, and the contribution of each campaign.

What metrics are right for your business? It can be a difficult question to tackle. Start by interviewing the executive team, the head of sales, and other key stakeholders. What types of information are they expecting from marketing? Executives really don't care about open rates, click-through rates, and page views. What data will be truly helpful to them? When in doubt, leave it out.

Of course, *you* should measure the impact of all key activities, but don't feel the need to report on anything that is not directly relevant to organizational decision-making (although it may be thoroughly advisable to track it for internal marketing purposes). Emphasize financial outcomes over marketing activities to aid in the transformation of the perception of marketing from a cost center to a revenue center. There are three major types of marketing analytics (key performance indicators—or "KPIs") that merit careful scrutiny:

- **Executive KPIs**—These are the stats that your executive team wants to see. They should cover the entire demand-generation spectrum. Some of the top choices include:

  - **Marketing-Sourced Leads and Opportunities**—How many leads are generated through marketing (someone who's *not* a customer)? What are their top channels and sources? How many opportunities in the pipeline were sourced by marketing?

  - **Marketing Contribution to Revenue**—How much of the revenue that closed during the period can be directly traced back to the campaigns and channels that marketing is responsible for?

  - **Marketing's Influence on Opportunities and Revenue**—Admittedly, this is a softer metric, but it's one that is gaining favor with marketing pros and business executives. If a sales rep generates a lead independently and enters it into the CRM system and marketing nurtures and engages with the lead, shouldn't marketing measure and report on the influence it has on educating the prospect *and* the effectiveness of the nurturing campaigns that the prospect experiences while continuing through the Demand Funnel? What about the recycle nurture? There's a key opportunity to show marketing's influence on reengaging what would have been lost opportunity.

- **Demand Funnel KPIs**—These metrics help us understand the *velocity* and *efficiency* of our Demand Funnel by showing us a few key stats:

- **Prospects/Contacts at each Stage of the Demand Funnel**—How many prospects entered each stage of the funnel during a given period and is this number trending up or down?

- **Stage Conversion Rates**—You want to report how many prospects move from one stage to the next. For example, what percentage of inquiries convert to MQLs? How many MQLs get recycled or move down the funnel and become SALs? Also, calculate "broad-jump" stats: How many leads convert from Inquiry to SAL, or from MQL to Closed/Won? If you have low conversion rates from Inquiry to MQL, maybe you're "fishing in the wrong spot" or using the wrong "bait." If you have low conversions from MQL to SAL, there might be an SLA problem (*i.e.* sales is taking too long to initiate/engage with the prospect or, more likely and common, you have a general CRM adoption issue by sales). And if your SAL-to-Opportunity conversion rate is low, it suggests a problem with the sales process, their selling skills, strong competition, pricing issues, or other problems worth investigating.

- **Average Time at Each Stage**—Measuring how long the average prospect spends in each stage tells you the velocity of your Demand Funnel. This data is especially helpful for comparing to prior periods.

- **Lead-Score Distribution**—Create a bar chart showing how many A, B, C, D, and E leads are in the system. This helps you assess the quality of your lead-scoring activities and whether your nurtures are successfully moving up the lower-ranked leads.